Redleaf *Quick* Guide

Developmental Milestones

OF YOUNG CHILDREN

Revised Edition

Karen Petty, PhD

Redleaf Press®
www.redleafpress.org
800-423-8309

Published by Redleaf Press
10 Yorkton Court
St. Paul, MN 55117
www.redleafpress.org

Revised edition 2016
Cover design by Jim Handrigan
Typesetting by Douglas Schmitz
Typeset in Signo
Printed in the United States of America

Library of Congress Cataloging-in-Publication Data

Names: Petty, Karen, author.
Title: Developmental milestones of young children / Karen Petty.
Description: Revised edition. | St. Paul, MN : Redleaf Press, [2016] |
    Series: Redleaf quick guide
Identifiers: LCCN 2015036081 | ISBN 9781605544793 (alk. paper)
Subjects: LCSH: Child development—Handbooks, manuals, etc. | Child
    psychology.
Classification: LCC HQ767.9 .P475 2016 | DDC 305.231—dc23
LC record available at http://lccn.loc.gov/2015036081

Printed on acid-free paper   U22-05

To my grandsons, Kason, Jay, Sam, and Zaidon, who have brought me more joy than I ever imagined and whose stages of development instructed and inspired my writing throughout this book.

CONTENTS

Introduction vii

How to Use This Book vii

Who Is This Book For? vii

Why Study the Development of Children? vii

The Caregiver and Development viii

Diversity viii

Domains of Development viii

Chapter 1: Observing Children 1

How to Use the Observational Record 2

Chapter 2: Documenting Milestones 5

Recording Observations through Documentation 7

Chapter 3: Communicating with Families 9

Partnerships with Families 9

Two-Way Communication with Families 9

Bringing Up Concerns 10

Basing Curriculum on Developmental Milestones 10

Chapter 4: Birth through Twelve Months 13

Physical and Motor Development 13

Social and Emotional Development 17

Communication and Language Development 19

Cognitive Development 20

Approaches to Learning 22

Chapter 5: One-Year-Olds 23

Physical and Motor Development 23

Social and Emotional Development 25

Communication and Language Development 26

Cognitive Development 27

Approaches to Learning 28

Chapter 6: Two-Year-Olds 31

Physical and Motor Development 31

Social and Emotional Development 32

Communication and Language Development 34

Cognitive Development 34

Approaches to Learning 36

Chapter 7: Three-Year-Olds 37

Physical and Motor Development 37

Social and Emotional Development 39

Communication and Language Development 42

Cognitive Development 43

Approaches to Learning 45

Chapter 8: Four-Year-Olds 47

Physical and Motor Development 47

Social and Emotional Development 48

Communication and Language Development 50

Cognitive Development 51

Approaches to Learning 53

Chapter 9: Five-Year-Olds 55

Physical and Motor Development 55

Social and Emotional Development 56

Communication and Language Development 58

Cognitive Development 59

Approaches to Learning 60

Chapter 10: Six-Year-Olds 61

Physical and Motor Development 61

Social and Emotional Development 62

Communication and Language Development 63

Cognitive Development 64

Approaches to Learning 66

Chapter 11: Seven-Year-Olds 67

Physical and Motor Development 67

Social and Emotional Development 68

Communication and Language Development 69

Cognitive Development 69

Approaches to Learning 71

Chapter 12: Eight-Year-Olds 73

Physical and Motor Development 73

Social and Emotional Development 74

Communication and Language Development 75

Cognitive Development 76

Approaches to Learning 77

Resources 79

Charts of Developmental Milestones 79

INTRODUCTION

Karen Petty, PhD

Benchmarks of development are important to all caregivers and families alike because they provide information that can help them observe and chart a child's development over time. While environments, child-to-adult ratios, caregiving routines, and group size are important for young children in care, knowledge of and attention to children and their development are most important. This book provides descriptions of developmental milestones, which are behaviors exhibited by children (and observed by caregivers) at certain times during their development from infancy through early school age. Educators also refer to these milestones as *developmental indicators*.

How to Use This Book

This book can be used as a caregiver's guide to the typical developmental milestones of children from birth through eight years. This book is *not* a diagnostic tool or a remedy for children with developmental delays or differing abilities. It is intended as a quick reference that can be used alone or in conjunction with the *Assessment of Developmental Progress: Birth to Age 8*, which can be ordered from the Redleaf Press website (www.redleafpress.org).

Who Is This Book For?

Parents frequently ask, "How will I know if my child is progressing normally?" or "Is my child keeping up with other kids his age?" The more caregivers know about young children and their stages of development, the less anxious and better prepared they are to care for children at any age or stage. Caregivers of young children—teachers, child care providers, families, and friends—will benefit from this book because the valuable information it contains will help them understand and know when a young child may need special care or diagnostics. It will also allow them to provide developmentally appropriate environments and activities for children in their care. While no measure of development can be considered definitive, some typical milestones are achieved universally by most children at particular ages and stages. Knowing that children develop along a continuum that is unique to each individual child, caregivers can use these general milestones to identify children who may be developing more slowly or more rapidly than average.

Why Study the Development of Children?

The more caregivers know about the children in their care, the better they will be able to provide appropriate experiences for them. Noticing behaviors such as an infant smiling when she hears a particular voice or a preschooler getting cranky each day after mealtime will give caregivers a sense of who the child really is. Small observations such as these further caregivers' knowledge of child development and their familiarity with and understanding of the individual children in their care.

The Caregiver and Development

To be a professional in the field of child development and the care of young children, caregivers need an understanding of the children in their care. They need to understand the domains of child development as well as the behaviors typical of children at a particular age. This book can be used as a source of information for families and others who care for children. As caregivers learn more and more about children and developmental milestones, their individual planning for each child will improve.

Diversity

Caregivers can make efforts to celebrate the diversity of children as members of a family unit and as individuals with specific characteristics that are all their own. Children are one-of-a-kind, and they come from families who represent diverse cultures, languages, abilities, and experiences. It is the caregiver's job to learn about each child's background in order to know each individual in a more sensitive and meaningful way.

Knowing the child means knowing the family. Connections to families can be made stronger and more meaningful when caregivers take the time to bring the diversity of families' lives into their own practice. After all, caregivers share the same goal with each family—for their child to succeed.

Domains of Development

There are many domains of development, but this book focuses on five:

- physical and motor development
- social and emotional development
- communication and language development
- cognitive development
- approaches to learning

Each domain is important in its own right but also works in tandem with the others. Children do not function in a single domain at a time. While children carry out their daily tasks, they often work in several or all of the domains concurrently. The five domains listed here are addressed for each age and each developmental stage throughout this book. They can look dramatically different from one age to the next. For example, a child's vocabulary skills at one year are dramatically different from a child's vocabulary skills at eight years. The domains help categorize the observed behaviors and milestones.

Karen Petty, PhD, holds a master's degree in early childhood education and a doctorate in curriculum and instruction with emphases in early childhood and child development. She has over twenty years of experience teaching and caring for young children and conducting trainings and workshops. Dr. Petty is a consultant for military installation family member programs and is the author of Deployment: Strategies for Working with Kids in Military Families. *She is a professor of early childhood development and education and chair of the Department of Family Sciences at Texas Woman's University in Denton, Texas.*

CHAPTER 1: OBSERVING CHILDREN

Observation is the best way to assess and document developmental milestones in young children. It takes skill to become an accomplished observer, but as a caregiver, you can better understand children—their behaviors, skills, knowledge, and feelings—if you watch and listen to them in focused and purposeful ways. The more you observe, the more you become aware of each child's unique abilities. As you conscientiously watch and listen to children, you can record what you observe and document their development. In addition to revealing much about children and their development, ongoing, focused observations can keep you centered on each individual child rather than only on those whose behaviors frequently command your attention. Observation is also an authentic way to systematically record children's behavior.

The Observational Record, which can be used with this book, is a good resource to help you maintain your focus, know what to look for, and know when each milestone may occur.

The Observational Record will help you maintain documentation of a child's development over time. By using the Observational Record, you will minimize your biases by concentrating on observing certain behaviors and skills rather than trying to decipher what you see. That is, instead of trying to interpret a child's behavior, you will simply record whether the child is in the *learning* stage of development, the *practicing* stage, or the *mastery* stage based on your observations. The notes column can be used to document factual details for each milestone you observe.

> You can download a PDF of the Observational Record from the Redleaf Press website. Go to www.redleafpress.org, type *observational record* into the Search box, and follow the links.

The *learning* stage occurs when a child experiences something for the first time or when a task is initially taught. For example, an infant first babbles and laughs between three to six months of age to get adult attention.

Children reach the *practicing* stage when they have been exposed to a new skill but haven't quite mastered it. As the caregiver or teacher, you should continue to provide the children with opportunities to learn the skill until they reach an "aha" moment and perform the skill or behavior on their own.

The *mastery* stage comes when children consistently perform or exhibit a behavior over a period of time without your assistance. For example, it would be premature to record mastery for the milestone "stands alone" if a one-year-old attempts to stand unassisted on one occasion and then does not attempt to stand alone for another month.

You can purposefully refer to the Observational Record and use your observations to plan opportunities for children to work toward each upcoming milestone. In this way, the Observational Record becomes an excellent planning tool. You can use your recorded observation to plan developmentally appropriate activities for the children in your care. Using observations to develop and modify curriculum is more appropriate then using a curriculum that may be unrelated to the developmental stages of the children in your care.

The Observational Record is an authentic assessment tool. This is different from a formal assessment, which tends to take a snapshot of a child's behavior or ability during a single incident. Using the Observational Record gives caregivers an opportunity to conveniently observe the child more than once and over time. It also allows more than one person to document and record what is observed, which provides greater validity to and consistency in the child's records. The most important reason to observe children, however, is to benefit them personally by providing their caregivers and families with a holistic look at their development in several domains over time, rather than in just one specific area at one specific time.

Authentic observation done informally in real settings may be the best way to chart children's progress, or lack thereof. It can be used to share information about the development of the children in your care as well as to provide evidence of how well children progress toward the outcomes or standards of your program. Your curriculum can be built on the authentic assessments you do with the children during their daily routines—indoor and outdoor play, group times, and learning activities—rather than during pullout testing and measurement or through standardized testing. The best observations of young children

- are based on knowledge of children and their development;
- occur in a child's natural environment;
- occur over time;
- are fact based and objective;
- look at individual children and their interactions with other children;
- are done by the child's caregiver or teacher;
- are based on strengths rather than weaknesses;
- are performance based;
- include samples of children's work.

How to Use the Observational Record

The developmental milestones found in this book and in the Observational Record that accompanies this book are important events in the lives of young children ages birth through eight years. They reflect the current research on children's growth and development. Along with the benefits discussed previously, the Observational Record can also provide an alert if a child is in need of additional or more in-depth assessments by outside observers, such as diagnosticians, doctors, and consultants. When the Observational

Record is used for activity planning and assessment, remember that the ages associated with each milestone are expected rather than definite. No child develops at the same rate as others. When using the assessment booklet,

- try to be discreet;
- observe during routines and activities;
- focus on a single domain of development at a time rather than trying to complete the whole checklist at once;
- concentrate on one child at a time;
- plan activities that foster behaviors and skills included in the assessment booklet;
- avoid making judgments or inferences about a child (be as unbiased and objective as possible);
- listen for words that are spoken and record them in the assessment booklet.

The Observational Record can display a lot of information at a glance that is easy to understand and interpret. Adults other than the observer/recorder can use the information to continue to track a child's progress. The records can be passed on to future caregivers in a child's portfolio. Along with samples of the child's work, the Observational Record gives a true picture of the growth and development of the whole child.

CHAPTER 2: DOCUMENTING MILESTONES

Learning about children comes from careful observations—listening to and watching them in authentic environments such as their classrooms. You can become a skilled observer who studies children and documents the important milestones they achieve over time. Documenting milestones is a two-step process: (1) collecting the information that is observed, and (2) recording it.

Your collection of information about young children should be based on focused observations of appropriate developmental milestones. The developmental milestones listed in this book can be used to guide your observations.

Recording what you observe is important, because it becomes a written record of the child's performance. It also allows you to save valuable information in a way that can be easily referenced; that is, you don't have to rely on your memory to know what the child can do. Based on the child's prior performance, you can create activity plans that are developmentally appropriate for individual children. This written record will also be a valuable tool when communicating with families.

Documentation can be used to show a child's progress through the stages on the developmental continuum—learning, practicing, and mastery—and can show patterns of growth such as sitting up, crawling, and walking in infants, or scribbling, controlled drawing, and writing in preschoolers. Additional benefits for documenting observed behaviors include

- assuring families you are committed to providing care based on the needs of their children;
- putting an emphasis on learning and development;
- expanding learning to higher-level thought processes;
- challenging the child to develop or extend skills;
- increasing your ability as a professional.

You can share your documentation of a child's progress with families during conferences and scheduled or impromptu meetings. Just knowing you conduct purposeful and focused observations for documenting purposes is reassuring and exciting to families interested in the continuing development of their child.

Systematically recording observations on particular days of the week and when developmental milestones occur can help you organize your observations. The emphasis of documentation should be on learning and development—looking at a child's strengths instead of weaknesses.

When recording observations, you should follow the guidelines for accurate and objective recording and note-taking:

- Record only facts; document what you see, not what you think is happening.
- Observe without interpreting.
- Use words that describe but do not judge.
- Use short phrases rather than complete sentences.

The Observational Record is organized by the five domains of development covered in this book—physical and motor, social and emotional, communication and language, cognitive, and approaches to learning. It provides a list of the milestones typically achieved in

- the first year of life;
- one-year-olds;
- two-year-olds;
- three-year-olds;
- four-year-olds;
- five-year-olds;
- six-year-olds;
- seven-year-olds;
- eight-year-olds.

Attention is given to each domain of development during each of the first nine years of life in order to assess the whole child rather than only one facet of the child. As you observe, you may find patterns of development. For example, you may observe that three-year-old Kya shows advanced language ability but not advanced physical and motor skills. This does not mean she won't someday excel in the physical and motor tasks; it just shows that at this stage in her development, she has achieved the mastery stage in the language domain while being at the practice stage in her physical/motor domain. It is important to document a child's ability over time through multiple observations. Recording three observations each year is advised, though you may wish to do more observations if you think them necessary.

Not all of the domains have equal numbers of milestones to observe and record because of the natural patterns of development found in children on the whole. For example, in the "birth to one year" category, the physical and motor development domain has many more observable milestones than do the other four domains. This isn't surprising, considering the extreme amount of physical and motor development that occurs during the first year of a child's life.

When you care for children and are not focused on documenting their milestones, you often see and watch children carefully but do not necessarily observe them. As you familiarize yourself with the Observational Record and the milestones in this book for the children in your care, you may begin to observe milestones you hadn't noticed when you were just watching. Over time, observation and documentation becomes easier (if not automatic) when milestones are encountered. Your documentation should include narratives using quotes from the children, objective facts, and other anecdotal information. Documentation can also include photos, video, and samples of children's work.

When you provide activities for the children in your care, make efforts to increase their learning to higher-level thought processes. Whenever possible, scaffold (or assist) children while they learn new tasks so they practice and eventually master them.

An added benefit that naturally occurs when you document observations is the expansion of your abilities as a professional. The children benefit, and you benefit, too, when you become more knowledgeable of young children and the milestones important for them to achieve.

Recording Observations through Documentation

Some caregivers keep clipboards nearby in order to make quick recordings of behaviors, and some use sticky notes or address labels to jot down observed skills or abilities. Others use index cards stuffed in apron pockets or charts posted behind cabinet doors to capture moments when children accomplish firsts. Still others plan activities around particular skills and keep the Observational Record handy to document comments about the children and dates of observations. No matter what recording method you decide to use, you need a thorough understanding of the developmental milestones prior to observing. It will make recording events easier. You may focus for a day on reporting one child's progress toward several milestones, or you may document a particular milestone for a group of children at once, such as "child skips with two feet" for all of the older preschoolers and young schoolagers in your care. You can devise your own systematic way of observing and documenting the achievement of milestones, but what is most important is finding a method that works best for you as an individual. *You* know when *you* can best observe and record the actions of the children in your care.

CHAPTER 3: COMMUNICATING WITH FAMILIES

Documenting milestones has a direct benefit for families when you observe, record, and share a child's progress. Quality care uses observation and documentation of children's abilities at its core. Because of increased public awareness of quality programs for young children, including infants and toddlers, your efforts to provide documentation of children's progress over time are vital to family communication and relationships. The best programs for young children are based on strong commitments to and partnerships with families, and this book offers much in the way of building those relationships.

The Observational Record can become an important document for you and children's families. When you share the Observational Record with families, they, too, can become empowered to observe their own children in ways that go beyond merely watching. Whether your care is center or home based, you can involve families in the process of documenting developmental milestones.

Partnerships with Families

Seek partnerships with families when you assess and document children's development. Communicate your observations and assessments of milestones with families, and listen to their stories. Share photos, art, drawings, narratives, anecdotes, and stories with families, and encourage them to share the same with you. When families perceive themselves as equal partners with caregivers, they are much more apt to participate in the assessment process. For example, you might say, "I'm seeing James getting up on all fours. It looks like he is preparing to crawl. Are you seeing this at home as well?" Meetings or conferences with families can become celebrations of what their children *can do*. Assure families that your purpose is not to diagnose their child but to share the ways they are growing and developing over time.

Two-Way Communication with Families

A mutual exchange of information about children's development between families and you, the caregiver, is much more advantageous than traditional one-way communication in which the caregiver does all the talking while the families listen. This isn't communicating. Families are valuable resources when it comes to their children, and it is commonly known that children benefit from positive relationships between their families and caregivers.

Maintaining an open dialogue can give much insight into children's development and can assist in the observation and documentation of milestones. While keeping the information gained through observation discreet and adhering to the ethics of privacy for each child, you can find ways to communicate effectively with families. The following are some common and popular forms of two-way communication:

- family-teacher conferences (scheduled, impromptu, or as necessary), ideally at least twice a year;
- phone calls from families to caregivers and from caregivers to families (scheduled and unscheduled);
- arrival and departure conversations.

To help families understand your observations, you can schedule a conference with each family to review your documentation and to let them know what you have observed and recorded. At the beginning of the year, you may want to plan an evening gathering where all families are invited to attend a tutorial to guide them through the Observational Record and ways you will be using it to document milestones. That way, all families can hear the same information and have the opportunity to ask questions and make comments or suggestions. Either way, families will be better informed and, as a result, may take steps to foster the skills required of their children to meet each milestone. Share the assessment booklet with families so they, too, can chart their child's performance in the home environment. Conferences can provide opportunities for sharing your and their observations while you work together to support the child's efforts. Families will welcome education in order to provide guidance and opportunities for children's skills to emerge at home. This united support system will benefit caregivers, families, and, most important, children.

Bringing Up Concerns

After carefully tracking children's behavior and development, you may begin to observe patterns that suggest developmental delays. Perhaps you have concerns about one or more domains of the child's development. This book can help you describe typical development to families and explain where a child is on the developmental continuum at a given point in time. Families depend on caregivers to monitor children's progress and to alert them of concerns. On the other hand, as a caregiver, you should not make specific diagnoses or give advice about truly problematic behaviors. If growth is not occurring, you can show documentation of where the child is, carefully avoiding biased language or hints of comparisons to other children the same age. Try to talk only about the child's lack of development since your last observation or based on developmental milestones common for children the same age. You may also provide families with additional information on where they can seek additional screening or support.

Basing Curriculum on Developmental Milestones

Educational decision making, such as curriculum and lesson planning, should be based on the systematic recordings you have performed. Your developmentally appropriate and sequenced curriculum can be the basis for the program you offer. The program, in turn, is based on developmental milestones for each age and stage of children's development. In a circular fashion, developmental milestones are the basis for the curriculum, and the progress made by individual children occurs because you offer activities based on milestones.

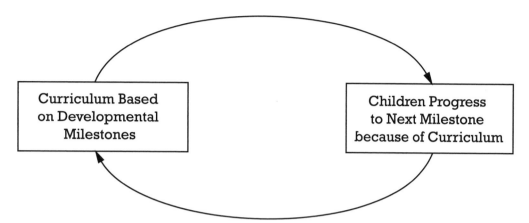

Outcomes can be favorable when you make a conscientious effort to provide experiences for young children that foster the development of milestones. For example, children who learn to write their names need experiences in holding crayons, markers, paintbrushes, and other instruments long before they begin penmanship. As a caregiver, you provide activities such as painting and drawing with multi-sized brushes and markers and give children opportunities to "write" often when they scribble their names and the names of their friends on papers of different sizes, textures, and colors. When you observe children to see if they have mastered the skill of writing their names, you improve their chances for success by preparing the environment.

CHAPTER 4: BIRTH THROUGH TWELVE MONTHS

During a baby's first year, remarkable changes occur in the five developmental domains: physical and motor, social and emotional, communication and language, cognitive, and approaches to learning. The developmental milestones in each of these domains are often referred to as *developmental indicators* and can be identified easily during your observations. Typically all babies achieve these common milestones, but they may do so at different rates. Even so, by the end of each stage of development, most babies will have reached the same developmental milestones. Keep in mind that the ages given are approximations, and infants may vary in their individual development and acquisition of skills.

Learning, practicing, and mastery are the three categories included in the Observational Record. The record provides three opportunities for infants to achieve mastery, though only one observation may be needed. As you observe, record a date and, if possible, a comment once you discover a milestone being attempted, repeated, or accomplished. And enjoy watching the babies!

Physical and Motor Development

Birth to Two Months

Exhibits a rooting reflex
Infants turn their heads (as if a bottle or breast is available) when their cheeks are stroked.

Reacts to loud noises
Infants appear startled or become quiet when they hear loud noises.

Holds head up
By the end of their first month, infants can briefly raise their heads from the shoulder of the person holding them or from a flat surface, such as a crib or the floor.

Makes quick and jerking arm movements
Infants don't have a completely developed nervous system at this time and continue to act using their reflexes.

Brings hands to face
Infants find their faces and may suck their thumbs or put their hands in their mouths for a sensory experience.

Moves head from side to side while on stomach

Infants appear to survey their environment while looking from side to side; this movement is often accompanied by grunting sounds.

Focuses on objects eight to twelve inches away

It has been said that the distance from a mother's arms to her face while nursing is about the same distance that an infant can gaze or focus. Most parents and caregivers also hold babies in front of them at about this same distance.

Two to Three Months

Turns head easily to both sides in supine (lying on back) position

While infants' neck muscles continue to strengthen, they turn their heads frequently.

Lifts head off surface from prone (face down) position for one to two seconds

Infants often practice this exercise for very short periods of time before they become fussy or tired. This is another method of building strength.

Follows moving object with eyes

This is sometimes referred to as *tracking;* infants enjoy watching an object move back and forth slowly. They usually like to watch faces more than objects. Infants may turn away once a face or object has become too familiar because of repeated exposure.

Responds to loud sounds

Infants may respond with startled motions or crying when exposed to loud sounds, such as vacuum cleaners, honking horns, or alarm clocks.

Grasps and holds objects briefly

Do not confused this with the grasping reflex. Infants seek toys and grasp them briefly before letting go.

Three to Four Months

Brings hands to midline while on back

Infants bring their hands to their midline when they explore and discover that they can control their hands.

Rotates or turns head from side to side with no head bobbing

Infants progress at this stage from head bobbing to more steady movements with no bobbing. While being held in an upright position, they may turn their heads from side to side while they explore the environment or hear sounds that interest them.

Holds head steady when carried or held

When infants are being held upright, they can hold their heads erect and steady.

Plays with hands and may hold and observe a toy

Infants can locate and play with their hands, often using them to grab and hold toys or nearby objects for a short time.

Reaches for objects

Infants' hand-eye coordination starts to develop. They notice toys that they want to hold and attempt to pick them up.

Pushes down on legs when feet are placed on a firm surface

Around four months of age, when infants are held in a standing position with their feet on a firm or hard surface, they appear to propel themselves to jump.

Exhibits the rooting reflex less often or not at all

As you stroke their cheeks, infants do not respond by turning their heads but by smiling or gazing at you.

Four to Six Months

Follows distant object with eyes

Infants' eyes work together and focus equally on objects; they can track objects' movement from a greater distance.

Lifts head while in supine (lying on back) position

Infants have developed strong neck muscles.

Holds chest up with weight on forearms

Infants are stronger in the upper chest area and can now support their weight with their forearms.

Rolls from stomach to side

This is infants' early attempt at rolling all the way over.

Rolls from stomach to back

This movement usually follows soon after infants learn to roll from their tummies to their sides.

Rolls from back to stomach

This movement usually follows infants learning to roll from their stomachs to their backs.

Stands with support

Infants can stand briefly if you hold them up. This exercise increases leg strength.

Brings feet to mouth easily while in supine (lying on back) position

Infants strengthen their upper body movements when they reach for, grab, and pull their feet forward to their faces. Doing this also helps them achieve a perception of self.

Six to Nine Months

Transfers object from one hand to another

After taking a toy, babies can move the toy back and forth at will.

Uses toes and hands to propel forward or in a circle

Babies dig in their toes and hands to move.

Attempts to crawl (stomach and legs dragging)

With their stomachs touching the floor and heads and shoulders supported by the weight borne by their elbows, infants pull along their bodies while their legs drag behind, as they do in swimming or kicking.

Crawls

Babies move on their hands and knees from one place to another at will.

Gets to a sitting position

Babies can pull themselves up into a sitting position independently.

Grasps small items

Babies use their whole hands, and they pick up small toys or objects with their thumbs and fingers.

Sits without support

Babies can sit unsupported in a high chair for feeding or on a solid, flat surface to play.

Can be pulled to feet but can't support self

Babies can support their body weight and stand on their feet with external support (adult hands, furniture, and so forth).

Nine to Twelve Months

May stand momentarily without support

In preparation for walking, babies continue to gain strength in their legs and lower body by standing often. Usually babies stand by holding onto something solid, such as a chair, low table, or sofa, and then let go of the object to take their first steps.

Walks with assistance

Babies delight in pretend walking, or prewalking, by holding onto adults' hands or surrounding furniture. They may walk briefly (two or three steps) without assistance.

Walks alone

Babies can walk unsupported on flat surfaces.

Social and Emotional Development

Birth to One Month

Makes demanding cries

Infants use loud, demanding cries to communicate with us. They may be hungry, wet, uncomfortable, or sick.

Shows sense of trust

Infants' sense of trust shows that they are nurtured and cared for in positive ways. Their demands and needs are met consistently and readily. Infants often show less tension and more stability when they can trust the adults around them.

Shows attachment (responds positively) to significant adults

Securely attached infants readily respond to tenderness and compassion from their caregivers.

Makes eye contact

Babies make eye contact for several seconds with their caregivers.

One to Three Months

Coos

Infants communicate by cooing or making gurgling or grunting sounds. Language and speech development occur when they attempt to socialize.

Smiles at the sound of familiar voices

Infants are born knowing the sounds of voices they have heard repeatedly while in utero. Many parents read to their unborn babies, and there is evidence that babies recognize their voices.

Tracks moving persons or objects

Infants have a developing curiosity and are attracted by movement. Their visual acuity develops during this activity.

Cries to demand attention

Infants continue to develop a sense of trust in others and use crying to get caregivers to meet their needs.

Smiles at strangers

Infants do not fear strangers at this age and often smile at unfamiliar faces.

Three to Six Months

Babbles and laughs to get adult attention

This vocal activity becomes more intentional at this age; infants seek interactions with important adults and other children.

Responds to smiles with smiling

Imitation of a smiling adult or sibling is common. Infants appear to smile when someone smiles at them.

Pays close attention to older children and their actions

Infants watch older siblings, especially older toddlers, and respond with occasional smiles.

Calms self

Infants can sometimes regulate their own distress by placing their fingers in their mouths or by focusing on something else, such as toys, clothing, or mobiles.

Looks and listens for purpose

Infants begin to understand that words and actions have meaning and look and listen attentively.

Six to Nine Months

Distinguishes voices of important, familiar people

Babies turn toward familiar voices and give them more attention by staring and moving their bodies in anticipation of communication.

Can distinguish voice tones and emotions

Babies can often tell when others are sad, happy, or angry by tone of voice. Caregivers can easily observe the way infants react to these emotions in adults.

Plays games with adults and older children

Games such as peekaboo and pat-a-cake are common, and babies appear to enjoy the element of surprise, as well as the close interaction with family members and caregivers.

Nine to Twelve Months

Begins to feel anxiety on separation from familiar adults (separation anxiety)

Babies start to cry or fuss when family members or caregivers leave their sight. They appear to notice the absence of significant persons.

Begins to feel anxiety in the presence of strangers (stranger anxiety)

When babies see unfamiliar people, they may begin to cry, cling to caregivers, or hide their faces.

Plays with others

Babies initiate social play, accompanied by laughter and high-pitched squeals.

Expresses emotions (happiness, sadness, anger, and surprise) through gestures, sounds, or facial expressions

Babies may display anger when they are denied goals or their goals are disrupted. At this age, anger has more purpose and is usually directed at something or someone in particular. Outbursts of slapping, kicking, knocking away, and stomping may accompany bouts of anger.

Explores environment

Once infants become mobile, they begin to use all of their senses to explore the environment around them.

Communication and Language Development

One to Two Months

Coos in response to adults' speech

Infants prefer human speech to other sounds. They respond by cooing to positive speech from adults.

Two to Four Months

Makes squealing and gurgling sounds

Infants learn to express themselves through vocalizations. Pretalking sounds, such as squealing and gurgling, also provide emotional outlets.

Four to Six Months

Babbles consonant sounds such as "ba-ba-ba-ba-ba" and "da-da-da-da-da"

Although many parents claim their children say "ma-ma" or "da-da" at this age, infants do not associate sounds with people at this stage of development.

Laughs out loud

Infants commonly laugh in response to tickles, smiles, gentle bouncing on adults' knees, and so on.

Six to Nine Months

Babbles sounds, such as "goo" and "gaa"

These sounds are a combination of vowels and consonants and are considered to be important prespeech behavior.

Experiments with vocalizations that include longer and more varied sounds

Babies yell or make loud, extended sounds when tired and "ahhhhhhhhh" or "ehhhhhhhhh" sounds when happy.

Uses intonations in sounds

Babies imitate the rise and fall of adult speech in their vocalizations.

Responds to own name

Babies turn their faces toward adults or children who speak the babies' names.

Develops receptive-language vocabulary

Babies understand simple words, commands, and phrases long before they can talk. They understand more words every day. Their receptive-language understanding is much larger than their expressive ability.

Nine to Twelve Months

Says at least one word

Babies make particular sounds associated with distinctive actions or objects, such as a cracker, cookie, blankie, or shoe. Adults may not understand the sounds, but the babies are likely to repeat them when they see those objects.

Gestures or points to communicate

Although babies don't talk, they may indicate their needs by reaching for objects. They may indicate they want to be held by reaching up to their caregivers.

Listens to songs, stories, or rhymes with interest

Babies enjoy being read to and pay attention to played or sung music.

Imitates sounds

At this time, most babies can say "Uh-oh!" in imitation of their family members or caregivers.

Cognitive Development
Birth to Two Months

Shows understanding that crying brings comfort

Infants whose cries are responded to in a timely manner appear to show a sense of trust that crying gets their needs met.

Prefers black-and-white or high-contrast patterns

Although this lasts for only about the first three months, most infants show a definite preference for these visual patterns.

Two to Four Months

Explores the environment with senses

Infants look, gaze, mouth, and turn their heads to sounds and textures in the environment.

Discovers hands and feet are extensions of self

Infants stare at their hands and intentionally grab or hold their feet.

Responds to own reflection in mirror

Infants are drawn to their own reflections. They make eye contact and may reach out to touch their reflections.

Anticipates events

Infants begin to recognize that a meal, a bath, or bedtime is about to happen.

Four to Six Months

Shows interest in manipulating toys and objects

Infants become more intentional in making their own selections during this period. They also grasp and hold onto objects for longer periods of time.

Six to Nine Months

Investigates objects by banging, shaking, and throwing

Babies explore cause and effect when they manipulate objects for a desired outcome or result.

Shows interest in objects with moving parts

Babies poke, prod, rattle, and bang toys with moving parts. They also like to watch moving mobiles and other hanging objects that gently sway when moved.

Shows interest in playing games

At about eight months, babies can initiate games that are familiar to them rather than wait for a caregiver or sibling to initiate them.

Nine to Twelve Months

Responds to "no"

Babies can shake their heads "no" in response to questions or commands from adults and may begin saying "no" soon afterward.

Waves bye-bye

With prompting, babies usually can wave at this age, but they sometimes wave without prompts.

Shows understanding of object permanence (that is, knows objects exist when out of sight)

Hide a toy underneath a blanket or behind a box, and babies search for it.

Engages in more intentional play

Babies may run a train along a track or place a ball in a basket.

Intentionally selects toys to play with

It is not uncommon for babies to crawl toward desired toys, persons, or objects.

Shows understanding that objects have purpose

Babies begin to purposefully or imitatively use objects, such as hairbrushes, telephones, and spoons.

Approaches to Learning

Birth to Six Months

Shows curiosity by exploring with senses

Infants have a developing curiosity and use all of their senses to explore the environment around them.

Six to Twelve Months

Shows persistence by repeating actions

When infants' actions create an effect, such as the sound made by banging on a drum, they begin to show persistence by repeating their actions again and again.

Explores the environment actively, regardless of obstacles

Infants love to explore using their whole bodies. Babies six to twelve months can overcome obstacles and emerge successful.

Intentionally looks for and reaches for objects of interest

Infants choose and reach for desired toys, objects, or persons.

CHAPTER 5: ONE-YEAR-OLDS

Between twelve and twenty-four months, young children are full of energy and seem to get into everything! Balancing on their feet and eventually walking are marked achievements at this stage of development. Beginning communication skills emerge as children become more adept at using language and start to develop a vocabulary. One-year-olds constantly seek interactions with other people (peers and caregivers), and as they approach twenty-four months, they develop a sense of self. While the following developmental milestones are common to all children ages twelve to twenty-four months, remember that children develop at different rates.

Physical and Motor Development

Twelve to Eighteen Months

Enjoys clapping hands

At age one, children can clap their hands in excitement or to mimic adults.

Walks with assistance

Most children walk during this stage without assistance, but some still cling to adults or to furniture when they venture out.

Begins to use a spoon

Young toddlers begin to grab spoons from their caregivers, as if to feed themselves, and eventually can move the spoon to and from their mouths.

Walks without assistance

One-year-olds can walk independently without the help of adults.

Crawls up and down stairs

Toward the end of this stage, twelve- to eighteen-month-olds can navigate stairs by crawling but need adults close by.

Stacks two objects

At age one, children can stack two objects, one on top of the other, using their new fine-motor skills.

Pulls off socks and shoes

By the end of their first year, young toddlers can take off socks and shoes but cannot put them back on. They can remove other things, such as their diapers, toys stacked on rings, and objects in a cabinet.

Likes to push, pull, carry, and dump things

Toys that young toddlers can push, pull, fill with things, carry, dump, and refill are their favorites. Toys such as balls, trucks, cars, and boxes are great to offer young toddlers.

Scribbles without control

One-year-olds scribble or move an object without purpose until they acquire more motor and visual control.

Eighteen to Twenty-Four Months

Walks up and down stairs with help

Toddlers begin to gain motor control. They have better coordination when they place one hand on a railing and the other in a caregiver's hand.

Walks on uneven surfaces with help

Sand, pebbles, sloping surfaces, and other uneven surfaces enable toddlers to gain greater balance with a caregiver's help. Falling down is natural, and within a few weeks, their control will increase as they walk without assistance.

Stands on one foot with help

Toddlers cannot stand alone on one foot because their balance has not developed at this age. They hold their arms high or close to their chests to help balance themselves.

Runs reasonably well

Toddlers may be a bit wobbly, but they soon master running (with occasional falls).

Rolls wheeled toys such as trains, cars, and trucks with ease

Young toddlers prefer toys that roll and that are easy to grasp when playing. Both smooth and flat or inclined surfaces are interesting playscapes for toddlers.

Throws a ball

Toddlers throw underhand at first and then progress to overhand throwing.

Can feed self

Finger foods and foods that can be spooned are of interest to toddlers. Grasping and pinching are preskills needed to hold writing tools and other objects.

Begins to dress self

At the end of this year, toddlers can usually put on their own shoes, socks, and hats.

May begin toilet training

Although toilet training often begins at this stage, it usually isn't mastered until the third year (age two). Girls generally train earlier than boys.

Social and Emotional Development

Twelve to Eighteen Months

Shows signs of attachment to parents or other family members
Toddlers twelve to eighteen months may cry briefly when left with caregivers.

Engages predominantly in parallel play with peers
At this age, toddlers usually play alongside other children but do not interact with them.

Begins to imitate older siblings or peers
Imitation is the basis of the role play and dramatic play that occur during children's third year (age two).

Shows signs of teasing adults
One-year-olds can tease adults by hiding their faces and then revealing them with a huge smile.

Shares toys or possessions
One-year-olds may begin to share toys or possessions occasionally. They are beginning to learn to empathize with others.

Understands the meaning of "no"
At twelve to eighteen months of age, children begin to stop their activities in response to the word *no*. Many times they resist directions and need to be physically removed from the situation.

Eighteen to Twenty-Four Months

Initiates separation from caregivers
Toddlers wander off from caregivers to explore or attempt to communicate with their peers.

Looks for "home base" or significant adult
Even with their new autonomy and independence, toddlers still need to know that caregivers are close by so they can venture out and retreat as often as necessary.

Plays with other toddlers
At this stage, play is mostly solitary but can include interactions with other toddlers—for example, to claim a toy or to make physical contact, as if to say, "Hi!"

Shows sense of trust
When toddlers ask to be picked up and held or cry because they are hungry or need to be changed, they show their trust that caring adults respond in a timely manner.

Shows attachment to significant adults

Caregivers are extremely important as sources of affection and safety to toddlers. You can observe secure attachment when caregivers leave the room and toddlers cry or when caregivers move close to toddlers and the children lean into the caregivers to be held.

Shows signs of stress when family members initiate separation

Toddlers notice when family members depart but cannot forecast when they will return. They live only in the moment.

Washes face and hands

Young toddlers can practice self-care, such as washing their faces and hands with adult assistance.

Shows increasing ability to cope with stress

Young children's ability to cope with stress increases with their positive social relationships to caregivers.

Communication and Language Development
Twelve to Eighteen Months

Uses gestures and actions intentionally

At this age, young toddlers point to get adults' attention, hold brushes to initiate having their hair brushed, or wave to say bye-bye.

Intentionally says "mama" and "dada"

At last, family members can know that their children are referring to them when they say "Ma-ma" and "Da-da." Prior to this stage, the sounds were just verbal utterances lacking reference to specific people.

Uses one sound to stand for more than one gesture or object

Early in this stage, one-year-olds develop sounds, such as "guh," to stand for "I want that," and then a few days or weeks later may use the same sound to stand for "That's mine." Later in this stage, they begin to use a single recognizable sound to replace a whole phrase, such as "bah-bah" for "Give me my bottle!"

Speaks in jargon or nonsense phrases

At this age, twelve- to eighteen-month-olds use speech that is meaningful only to them. They commonly string together vowels and consonants when they point to or move toward an object of interest. These behaviors are known as *prespeech*.

Understands many more words than can be expressed

Young toddlers usually know the meaning of more words, especially nouns such as *brother, mama, ball, dog,* and so on, than they can pronounce. Some children do not talk much until the end of their second year, but when they do begin to talk more frequently, their language use erupts and they add many words daily to their speech.

Understands and responds to simple directions

Young toddlers can listen to and respond to simple directions, such as "Wave bye-bye" and "Bring the bucket to the table."

Eighteen to Twenty-Four Months

Says "hi," "bye," and "uh-oh"

Toddlers possess expressive vocabularies that usually receive attention, approval, or praise from significant adults.

Begins to express feelings with words

Toddlers use words like *sad, ouch,* and *mad* to verbally express themselves. "Me sad" or "Eva so mad" are examples of toddlers' first attempts to affirm their feelings.

Uses two- to three-word phrases

Older toddlers become skilled at putting words together in ways that make sense to them. They can get their needs met in the presence of adults. "Eat now!" and "We go home" are examples of early expressions.

Has a vocabulary of twenty to three hundred words

Vocabulary increases on a daily basis for children in this age group. Typical vocabulary at this age consists of between twenty and three hundred words.

Cognitive Development

Twelve to Eighteen Months

Tracks a toy that is being moved and can retrieve it if it's in partial view

At this stage, young children comprehend that objects like toys exist even if they are partially hidden.

Closes doors

Exercising cause and effect, one-year-olds can close (often slam) open doors but cannot reopen them.

Follows simple commands from adults or older children

Young toddlers can follow simple commands like "Put the book on the shelf" and "May I have the spoon, please?" Caregivers use such requests to engage young children in thinking, cooperative behavior, listening, and language development.

Turns pages in books

One-year-olds will become interested in books if adults read to them often. Without assistance, they may select and look at books they've seen before and may turn its pages.

Eighteen to Twenty-Four Months

Begins to recognize colors

Toddlers can identify the colors of objects by pointing or touching them before they can name the colors.

Enjoys container play

Toddlers enjoy putting objects into containers and using nesting toys.

Recognizes own image in a mirror

Toddlers smile, pat mirrors, and visit them many times as if to reaffirm their own reflections.

Approaches to Learning

Twelve to Eighteen Months

Focuses on some activities of interest

Young toddlers' attention spans gradually increase. Between twelve and eighteen months, children can focus on activities of interest for several minutes at a time.

Takes initiative, such as looking for a missing toy

One-year-olds begin to take initiative, especially with adult encouragement. Imaginative play becomes increasingly important at this stage.

Shows creativity by using objects in new ways

At this age, young children actively explore. They may experiment with objects many ways before finding uses for them. For example, they may wear bowls on their heads as hats.

Eighteen to Twenty-Four Months

Shows curiosity in daily experiences and activities

Toddlers have a growing sense of curiosity. When they engage in new experiences and activities, they often ask questions like "Why?" and "What's that?"

Willing to try new activities and experiences

Toddlers are open to risks and new or unfamiliar activities, as long as they have the help and support of trusted adults.

Increasing interest and independence in completing simple tasks

As their skill levels increase, toddlers can complete simple tasks, often without adult assistance. Older toddlers are also interested in learning to do things for themselves.

Shows interest in activities, people, and the environment for a short period of time

As children approach the age of two, their attention spans increase. Toddlers show interest in activities, people, and their surroundings for longer periods of time than during infancy.

Expresses choices and preferences

Toddlers possess definite preferences and can make choices based on those preferences. Allowing young children to make structured choices increases their independence and self-confidence.

Repeats activities many times to begin to achieve mastery

As their skill levels rapidly increase, toddlers repeat the same activities several times, improving their abilities and achieving mastery.

CHAPTER 6: TWO-YEAR-OLDS

The third year of life is a period of transition between being toddlers and preschoolers, and children make much progress in all areas of development. Many move out of their cribs and into their own beds. They make choices about what to play with, what to wear, and what to eat. They begin to express their emotions and voice opinions. Their physical and verbal abilities increase rapidly, and their need for caregivers to keep them safe is greater than ever before. They enjoy routines, such as bathing, toothbrushing, and story time, before bed. Peers and siblings are important to them: they continue to play alongside them but not with them yet. Interactions with adults are essential for toddlers to begin to acquire a much-needed vocabulary and become independent preschoolers. While the following developmental milestones are common to all children at age two, remember that children develop at different rates.

Physical and Motor Development

Rides four-wheeled toys with ease

Toddlers can propel themselves backward and forward on riding toys.

Runs with ease

Toddlers seldom fall at this age unless they bump into something.

Stands on tiptoes

Many toddlers walk on their tiptoes or attempt to reach things by standing on their tiptoes.

Hammers

Many toddlers favor toy workbenches; they like to use plastic hammers to drive plastic nails and screws. They also tend to hammer with spoons—and just about everything else.

Engages in exercise play

Activities involving running, climbing, jumping, and chasing are popular with older toddlers; boys tend to engage in this type of play more than girls.

Shows interest in toilet training

Toddlers show more initiative to potty train at this age and because they are physically more developed, they are likely to succeed.

Opens doors by turning knobs or handles

Areas that were off limits to toddlers before are open for exploration because they can now turn most doorknobs and handles.

Turns the pages of a book (one at a time)

Two-year-olds have the small-motor skills to turn the pages of a book one at a time rather than handfuls of pages at once.

Has developed a hand preference

Most toddlers prefer to use either their right or their left hand by this time. Occasionally they switch hands when coloring or moving objects, but they usually prefer a particular hand for most tasks.

Holds markers and crayons with ease

Toddlers show more interest in writing utensils at this age and tend to write or mark on any surface.

Uses paint, clay, and dough

Most toddlers enjoy using different media to paint, roll, pound, and sculpt.

Stacks toys with ease

Building blocks, boxes, and other items are of interest to toddlers, who try to stack them (usually taller than themselves) until the stack falls.

Shows an interest in drawing and marking

Older toddlers make squiggles and draw shapes, such as circles and rectangles, at this stage.

Is toilet trained

Toddlers may continue to have accidents, even after being toilet trained, and may still require diapers at naptime or bedtime.

Rides a trike

Peddling is much easier now, and toddlers often alternate between propelling a trike with their feet and using the pedals.

Social and Emotional Development

Shows independence in bathing, brushing teeth, dressing, and selecting clothing

With self-sufficiency in sight, toddlers practice self-care with little assistance from adults.

Is interested in anatomy

At this stage of development, toddlers are aware of different body parts and often show curiosity about the anatomy of adults and peers by touching or staring.

Has tantrums

Toddlers at this stage of development explode emotionally when something is withheld from them.

Engages in parallel play

Most toddlers continue to play alone, but they often like to play alongside their peers.

Can identify and talk about personal feelings

Most older toddlers correctly use words, such as *scared, fun, funny,* and *feel bad* (among others), to describe their feelings. They can also remember and refer back to times when they felt mad or sad.

Can identify and talk about others' feelings

Older toddlers recognize the feelings of others and talk about their own emotions. Older toddlers also understand some of the needs of others and may attempt to help them or tell someone else about them by saying, for example, "Why is she sad?" or "Who hurt her?" (This ability to read the emotions of others should not be confused with empathy.)

Shows interest in helping

Older toddlers can assist adults and peers with some everyday tasks, such as setting the table for dinner, folding clothes from the laundry basket, and putting on a nighttime diaper. Toddlers also can put away toys at this stage of development, sometimes with assistance from peers or adults.

Can recite rules but cannot follow them consistently

Although older toddlers can verbalize rules, they don't always follow them.

Shows pride in accomplishments (especially physical)

Toddlers learn new skills and accomplish goals each and every day. At the age of two, young children show pride in their accomplishments, especially physical ones.

Begins to show respect for other people and possessions

Toddlers are aware of other people and begin to show respect for others' personal space and possessions, although they still may need an occasional reminder from an adult.

Is interested in the outside world

Two-year-olds show interest in what is happening in the world around them. Watching the garbage truck pick up trash or the mail carrier drop off mail can be very exciting to them.

Communication and Language Development

Shows an interest in print and books

Toddlers show the most interest in picture books (board books or paper books) at this age but also enjoy rhyming books, which they can recite in whole or in part.

Begins to use private speech

Toddlers can use language to direct their actions or intentions and do not require interactions from others. For example, they can say, "Jay's turn" when Jay takes his turn. Toddlers at this stage tend to say what they are thinking and about to do.

Shows ability to use naming words for objects of interest

Toddlers can use words such as *stegosaurus* appropriately if they have a high interest in dinosaurs.

Puts nouns and verbs together in simple sentences

"I do it" and "Her hit me" are examples of toddlers' expressions at this stage of development.

Echoes questions

Adult: "Where are your shoes?" Child: "Where are my shoes?"

Uses understandable speech

At 30 to 36 months, toddlers use mostly understandable speech, although correct grammar may not be used.

Uses a loud and soft voice

When speaking, older toddlers use different volumes, such as whispering, shouting, and soft conversational speaking.

Understands most things said by others

As their vocabularies increase, two-year-olds understand most things said by others, including caregivers, parents, and siblings.

Cognitive Development

Pretends to read

Toddlers want to hear stories over and over again and may pretend to read them or imitate adults who have read them out loud by repeating words or phrases from the book.

Can do simple sorting

Toddlers can sort blocks or other toys by two colors as well as sort familiar objects by twos—shoes and socks, for example.

Recognizes and names colors

Toddlers first learn basic colors, such as red, blue, black, and green. Some toddlers easily learn the names of other favorite colors, such as pink or purple.

Repeats simple nursery chants and rhymes

Toddlers often chant simple rhymes, such as "Twinkle, Twinkle, Little Star," "This Old Man," and many others they have learned at home and in care.

Sings parts of simple songs

Toddlers like songs that are repetitious, rhyming, and silly. They often sing parts of songs they can remember and make up silly songs that have no meaning.

Shows an interest in shapes

Toddlers find that shapes are interesting and challenging to learn. They usually can identify circles first and then rectangles. Older toddlers can draw circles; rectangles follow soon after.

Engages in more pretend play

Older toddlers use toys and objects to pretend with caregivers and other children.

Uses the word *no*

No! is such a powerful word. Toddlers use it to attempt to regulate their world and themselves.

Can talk about books

Older toddlers can name objects in books that have been read to them and relate the book's story to real events.

Can tell own age

Toddlers may recite their age when asked how old they are, saying "I'm two," for example.

Knows first and last name

Older two-year-olds may recite their whole name, particularly if their families spend time teaching them this concept.

Recalls past experiences

In conversations, older toddlers often refer to something that has happened in the past as "yesterday."

Asks questions

"Who's that?" "Where did Daddy go?" and "Where's his mommy?" are typical questions asked by older toddlers.

Creates imaginary friends

Older toddlers often pretend that stuffed animals and dolls are imaginary friends and may name them.

Follows more complex commands from adults

Toward the end of this year, a toddler can follow two-step directions, such as "Get your socks and bring them to me."

Approaches to Learning

Shows curiosity and interest in actively exploring the environment

Two-year-olds are very persistent and actively show interest and curiosity in their surroundings.

Shows pleasure in completing tasks

Toddlers commonly react to completing tasks with a sense of accomplishment and pleasure.

Maintains attention to complete a short, simple task with adult support

Throughout this year, toddlers' attention spans continue to increase. They can now complete simple tasks independently.

Insistent about preferences and may say "no" to adult

Once toddlers develop preferences for certain activities, routines, and objects, they insist upon those preferences and respond with "No" to objects or circumstances that challenge those preferences.

Demonstrates an understanding of cause and effect

Two-year-olds spend a great deal of their play examining cause and effect. These include dumping and filling buckets, turning lights on and off, and pushing buttons on toys to initiate sounds or actions.

Uses trial and error to solve more complex tasks or problems

Two-year-olds are beginning to use trial and error to solve problems: they make up words to a song or turn puzzle pieces in different directions to fit them into place.

CHAPTER 7: THREE-YEAR-OLDS

Now in their fourth year of life, three-year-olds have left infancy and toddlerhood and are now *young preschoolers.* These children are filled with the need to explore their worlds using all of their senses. They spend most of their time watching, imitating, observing, and doing. Physical growth slows, and they no longer have infantlike protruding stomachs and poor posture. Instead, young preschoolers are taller, thinner, and more adultlike. Three-year-olds enjoy repeating physical activities over and over, such as sliding, jumping, and riding a trike.

Social and emotional development in three-year-olds blossoms when they engage in silly behaviors and act in funny, precocious ways. With adults and peers as their audience, three-year-olds never run out of material. They begin developing a sense of humor that makes them a pleasure to be around. As language flourishes, three-year-olds explore words and their power, when used in certain ways. They like to tell others what to do and make plenty of demands. Three-year-olds have favorite words and like to repeat them, making sounds that may be irritating to adults but funny to them. They are great storytellers and like to be read to. Cognitively, three-year-olds get better at noticing differences and similarities in real objects, at matching, and at discovering patterns, textures, and lines in the environment. Overall, their wonderment and imaginations make them interesting and enjoyable to care for. While the following developmental milestones are common by the end of children's third year, remember that children develop at different rates.

Physical and Motor Development

Swings arms when walking
Three-year-olds are much more balanced and swing their arms in a rhythmic pattern when they walk. When they first began to walk, they held their arms lower.

Jumps with both feet
Three-year-olds can now steadily jump up when standing or jump down from a step or other low object and land on both feet without falling.

Rides three-wheeled toys
Three-wheeled toys such as trikes are a favorite of three-year-olds. Older three-year-olds can master them easily if the trikes are appropriately sized.

Walks on a balance beam or line
Three-year-olds can navigate a wide beam low to the ground or walk on a straight or curved line on the floor. These midline exercises are important for gaining whole-body coordination.

Balances or hops on one foot

Three-year-olds can hop on one foot briefly and may change from one foot to the other while doing so.

Slides without assistance

Older three-year-olds can climb a small slide with ease and slide down it without help from an adult.

Throws a ball (or another object) overhand

Three-year-olds can throw to a peer or an adult (or at a target) but often throw at nothing in particular and then retrieve the ball, repeating the exercise again and again with pleasure.

Bounces a ball and catches it

Older three-year-olds can bounce a ball and catch it with increasing precision.

Runs consistently without falling

In open spaces, three-year-olds run more often than walk and consistently maintain their balance, with only occasional falls.

Builds and stacks with several small blocks

Young preschoolers can build small towers with five to ten blocks or cubes. They delight in building, watching structures fall down, and rebuilding.

Pounds pegs with mallet

Three-year-olds can spend several minutes (ten to fifteen) pounding pegs into a board with a large mallet.

Copies and draws simple shapes and letters

Three-year-olds seek opportunities to draw simple shapes, such as circles and squares, or to copy drawings of shapes or letters.

Practices zipping, snapping, fastening, and buttoning

Three-year-olds attempt these skills but usually do not master them until their fifth year.

Can use scissors

Cutting with scissors is a desired skill for young preschoolers, and by the end of their third year, they are becoming proficient at cutting paper with child-sized scissors.

Makes marks or strokes with brushes, pens, pencils, and markers

Young preschoolers begin to hold and use marking tools in meaningful and creative ways to paint, write their names, copy, and draw.

Attempts to dress self

Independent three-year-olds attempt to dress themselves but still have difficulty with tying shoes, buttoning, and zipping.

Begins to stay dry while sleeping

Older three-year-olds can sleep through most nights without bed wetting, although they may have occasional accidents.

Naps less frequently

Three-year-olds typically sleep ten to twelve hours at night now and may need rest time, rather than full naps, during the day. Many three-year-olds continue to nap in programs where the schedule is very busy and tiring.

Completes toilet training

During their third year, young preschoolers use the toilet as needed and no longer wear pull-ups or training pants during the day.

Social and Emotional Development

Shows independence

Young preschoolers show independence when they say, "I can do it myself!" You recognize and encourage their need for independence when you offer limited choices, allow them to make mistakes, and encourage their accomplishments.

Engages in solitary play

Three-year-olds still sometimes prefer to play alone—for example, when they use a favorite toy or engage in a special activity. Their inconsistent voluntary sharing is one reason why playing alone may be preferred.

Engages in parallel play

Three-year-olds are sometimes comfortable playing in the vicinity of peers but not directly with them.

Begins to engage in associative play

Older preschoolers start to associate with peers on a limited basis, joining them when activities are alluring and they feel safe.

Plays with familiar peers often

Three-year-olds can pick up where they left off with familiar peers. They spend little time warming up and start to play immediately in most instances.

Plays with unfamiliar peers

Three-year-olds often play with unfamiliar peers on playgrounds or in restaurant play spaces when a family member is nearby.

Enjoys playing with adults as well as peers

Young preschoolers often seek playtime with adults and attempt to engage them in their pretend play. They often ask something like, "Will you play with me, Grammy? You can be the sister."

Begins to show perspective taking

Three-year-olds start to notice the feelings of others and may offer assistance. You can help them by pointing out others' feelings: "Shawn looks sad. Let's ask him if he needs our help." Doing so helps instill perspective taking.

Likes praise

Young preschoolers respond to praise when you show delight or excitement in their achievements. "You put the toy away all by yourself!" and "Look how you climbed up all by yourself!" are appropriate because they praise children's actions rather than the children.

Begins turn taking

Turn taking has been very difficult before now, but young preschoolers can take turns with your assistance. Set up situations where turn taking can be practiced, such as painting at an easel or riding the three-wheeler on the playground.

Shares

Three-year-olds continue the difficult task of learning to share. Toys, attention from adults, and favorite objects have been "mine" until now. Take it slowly, and give children lots of opportunities to practice. Teach the word *share,* and then use and model it often.

Begins to express feelings/emotions with words

At this age, young preschoolers talk about how they feel and identify emotions with words, such as *mad*, *sad*, *happy*, and *scared*. Use these terms often to help three-year-olds recognize emotions and learn to deal with them. Giving feelings a name can help children identify their feelings.

Is happy most of the time

Three-year-olds tend to be happy most of the time because they can self-soothe by playing independently or by asking an adult for help.

Enjoys helping with household tasks

More than at any other age, three-year-olds delight in helping with household tasks. They love to sweep, dust, turn on the dishwasher, help with cooking, and load the washing machine. Allow them to assist as often as possible, in care or at home. Their sense of independence and helpfulness can grow.

Likes to be silly and to make others laugh

Young preschoolers' senses of humor develop rapidly, and they delight in making others laugh by telling nonsense stories. They love to hear silly stories from adults as well and often imitate the stories to continue the laughter.

Begins to understand some limits and rules

Three-year-olds can sometimes be redirected with teaching statements, such as "I know it's hard to get dressed, but we have to wear warm clothes when we go out in the cold. Choose the socks that will keep your feet warm." Even during hurried moments, caregivers can engage young preschoolers in simple decision making rather than forcing them to comply.

Begins to seek adult attention and approval

Young preschoolers may be eager to please adults and may sometimes offer to help you by bringing a needed object or exclaiming, "Here, I made this for you!"

Shows fear

Three-year-old children's sense of what is real and what is unreal is not wholly developed. They often express a fear of monsters and other frightening characters they see on television, in movies, or in books. They may also express a fear of being left in unfamiliar surroundings by a family member.

Cries easily

At age three, crying means something different than when children were two. They can now use crying as a means to an end—to obtain something or to make something happen. Unmet physical or social and emotional needs are often the reason for the crying. If you can determine whether it is a physical need (hunger, exhaustion, wet or soiled clothing, or thirst, for example) or a social and emotional need (frustration, boredom, anxiety, sadness, anger, or fear, for example), you can better soothe three-year-olds.

Begins to understand danger

Young preschoolers can understand that playing on stairs or in the street is dangerous. Introduce the word *careful*, and use it often when discussing danger and how to avoid it.

Knows own gender and that of others

Three-year-olds recognize gender and can tell you their own gender. They can recognize likenesses and differences in the community, including "boyness" and "girlness."

Says "I love you" without prompting

Whether they imitate adults or initiate the statement themselves, three-year-olds now verbalize a loving connection to significant adults.

Makes simple choices (between two objects)

Young preschoolers start to choose between two objects, such as sandals or tennies. Keep their choices to a minimum for ease and to build self-esteem.

Engages in pretend play

"I'm a big green monster, and I'm gonna eat you up!" Three-year-olds spend a lot of time engaged in fantasy play and often enlist adults to play along.

Communication and Language Development

Speaks when spoken to

Young preschoolers start to understand and engage in back-and-forth conversation. When adults or other children speak to them, they can respond on their own. Their responses may make sense or seem nonsensical to you.

Tells stories without prompting

Referring to a child-sized drum, three-year-olds say, "This is my super wheel that my daddy's gonna drive and take me with him."

Enjoys rhymes and songs

Three-year-olds show more awareness than they did when they were two when adults sing songs and recite rhymes. Three-year-olds may not participate in singing or reciting, but they may sing later without prompting.

Likes to learn new words

When adults use new words conversationally, young preschoolers begin to make meaning of the words and start to use them in meaningful sentences.

Asks questions

Three-year-olds start to ask questions, such as, "Where you going?" and "Can I have one of those?" They also make statements that act as questions, such as "I'm hungry" for "Can I have something to eat?" They can respond to questions asked by others with *yes* or *no* answers.

Speaks in three- or four-word sentences (young three-year-olds)

"My mom is coming" is an example of a sentence that young three-year-olds can say. They may abbreviate their speech by leaving out small words, such as *are* in "Where you going?"

Uses up to seven words in sentences (older three-year-olds)

As they grow, three-year-olds start to sound more sophisticated; their speech becomes more like that of the adults around them. Young preschoolers catch on quickly and make correct sentences of their own, especially if caregivers model appropriate words and sentences, keeping their language simple and direct.

Begins to use correct grammar (syntax)

Adults can nurture the grammar ability of three-year-olds by constantly engaging in conversations with them, using words in grammatically correct ways. Caregivers can talk about things in children's world that are of interest to them, modeling appropriate and grammatically correct short sentences (five to seven words).

Understands the meaning of most preschool words (semantics)

Words that are commonly used in child care settings should be understood by young preschoolers. Three-year-olds can easily understand words such as *gecko* and *cottontail* if these animals are in their classrooms.

Uses language socially (pragmatics)

Older three-year-olds start to practice problem solving by (1) making requests ("Miss Julie, can I have a cookie?"), (2) being persuasive ("Will you play with me?"), (3) greeting others ("Hi, Mr. Lee!"), and (4) giving information ("In a minute").

Enjoys books that have photographs of real things

Photographs of animals and people are a must to three-year-olds. Adults can add to children's budding vocabulary by talking about the pictures with them, introducing new words like *calves* or *goslings*.

Enjoys picture books

Young preschoolers love books about dinosaurs going to bed as humans do, as well as books about caterpillars turning into butterflies.

Enjoys singing simple, repetitive songs

Music assists in developing language in three-year-olds because it is structured, repetitive, and predictable. New words and concepts can be developed through music as well as the ability to hear rhyming words.

Cognitive Development

Can stay with the same activity for five to ten minutes (increasing concentration)

Three-year-olds' ability to concentrate on self-chosen activities increases.

Uses toys to symbolize real objects

Young preschoolers can draw on their experiences and visualize them through the use of toy props. Hollow blocks can become cars to drive to the store. Toy shopping carts can be used to carry pretend food that can be cooked in a pot for dinner in the play-kitchen area.

Engages in fantasy play

"Here's some ice cream" (*an adult hands imaginary ice cream to a child*). "Thanks" (*the child pretends to eat*). "You can have the other ice cream" (*the child hands imaginary ice cream to the adult*). Three-year-olds can be prompted to engage in fantasy play, and the play can be extended when peers or adults pretend with three-year-olds.

Uses real objects as props during pretend play

Once older three-year-olds develop more abstract thinking, they can use a box to represent a birthday cake or a hollow block to represent a boat. Both now represent real-life experiences they are familiar with.

Puts interlocking puzzles together

Young preschoolers move away from knobbed puzzles and can put together multi-piece puzzles. They enjoy puzzles with pictures of the pieces printed in the puzzle tray, but now they enjoy ones with ten to twelve pieces, which makes them more challenging.

Begins to notice patterns

An important skill for three-year-olds is to notice patterns. This is the foundation for math and reading. The simplest pattern is *AAAAA* or *button, button, button, button, button.* "Look, Keri, it repeats over and over." *ABABAB* is another familiar, simple pattern that many three-year-olds can identify—red, blue, red, blue, red, blue, for instance.

Can sort or describe objects by one or more attributes

Attributes like size, color, shape, texture, and number become important to three-year-olds because they start to discriminate likenesses and differences between objects and to recognize the properties of the objects in their world.

Shows an interest in numbers and names of numbers

Three-year-olds start to show an interest in numbers at the point when they say, "I'm three" and "We live at 223 Blake Street." Most young preschoolers can recite numbers in order to 10 (and beyond) by the end of their third year and can count up to five objects, using one-to-one correspondence.

Uses words for time such as *yesterday* and *today*

Older three-year-olds become more oriented in time and often use words such as *yesterday* and *tomorrow* correctly (and sometimes incorrectly: "We are going to the park yesterday.")

Uses color names appropriately

By the end of their third year, young preschoolers often use basic color names in context. They may also use the name of other colors (favorites). "Look, Mai, you have red and I have red. But I really like pink."

Recognizes name in print

Three-year-olds can usually recognize their first names in print.

Identifies and names body parts

Three-year-olds know major body parts, such as eyes, ears, nose, mouth, hands, feet, and tummy.

Uses positional terms

Young preschoolers commonly use terms such as *over, under, above, inside,* and *outside.* Their clear understanding of these words help them use these words correctly. "My ball rolled under that tree" and "Let's go outside to play" are common uses of positional terms.

Names simple shapes

Three-year-olds can identify and name simple shapes, such as *circle* or *square.*

Has increasing memory

Young preschoolers possess greater memories and may be able to recall events from the past.

Approaches to Learning

Begins to purposefully explore new things or ideas

Three-year-olds ask a lot of questions and spend a great deal of time exploring new things and ideas. Adults can support their natural curiosity by encouraging them to try new experiences.

Approaches situations with increasing flexibility

Young preschoolers develop their problem-solving skills, increasing their flexibility. Adults can begin to rationalize with children who are three.

Invents new purposes for objects

Three-year-olds can think more abstractly, so they can invent new purpose for existing objects. For example, they may use a spoon as a microphone to sing a song.

Begins to create stories, imagining and describing things or situations that do not exist

Three-year-olds start to use their imaginations when they tell stories or describe situations. They may have an adventure on a pirate ship or take a trip to the moon and back.

CHAPTER 8: FOUR-YEAR-OLDS

Four-year-olds, or *preschoolers* or *prekindergartners,* are a pleasure to care for. They are funny, imaginative, energetic, silly, and often impatient. Their budding independence can be seen in their improved eating and dressing skills. Once their eye-hand coordination improves, they start to develop reading and writing skills. Their physical and motor abilities also improve, preparing them for gross-motor movements that continue to develop their running, jumping, hopping, throwing, and climbing skills. Socially, four-year-olds need opportunities to explore, investigate, and talk about the world around them. As they move out of toddlerhood, they rely less and less on adults and enjoy spending time with other children their same age. They sometimes appear fearless, but when they try to differentiate between what is real and what is fantasy, they may cling to adults.

Preschoolers' vocabulary increases daily. Culture has a big influence on the words they hear and begin to know. Cognitively, preschoolers are extremely curious and ask a lot of questions. It is not uncommon for them to begin their sentences with *who?, what?, where?,* or *why?* Enjoy their newfound independence and ability to verbalize their feelings when you care for four-year-olds. Each day, they will delight you with their silly stories and ability to engage you in their world. While the following developmental milestones are common by the end of their fourth year, remember that children develop at different rates.

Physical and Motor Development

Dresses with little assistance
By the end of this year, four-year-olds can sometimes tie their shoes and get dressed with much less help from adults.

Runs with ease and stops quickly
Four-year-olds become more agile and can run without falling or tripping. They can stop quickly when they play chase and tag.

Throws a ball with more accuracy and distance
Older preschoolers can throw farther and with more precision, and they often play catch with peers or adults. They develop their eye-hand coordination and their large muscles by throwing overhand and underhand.

Pedals and steers preschool-sized three-wheelers with ease
Four-year-olds have mastered three-wheelers and have fewer accidents. They can turn corners and steer out of the way of objects and peers.

Begins to pedal and steer a two-wheeled bike with training wheels

Older preschoolers develop physically at a fast pace. Many of them graduate to two-wheelers.

Puts puzzles together with ease

Preschoolers no longer need knobbed puzzles because they can use their pincer grasp with puzzles of twelve to eighteen pieces. Their prereading, writing, and problem-solving abilities develop when they choose pieces based on colors and shapes.

Copies, prints, cuts, pastes, and paints with a paintbrush

Older preschoolers can copy some simple shapes and use child-sized scissors and glue for simple projects. Their ability to paint with brushes increases, and by the end of their fourth year, they can easily hold writing and painting utensils using a tripod (three-finger) grasp.

Writes own name

By the end of their fourth year, preschoolers can usually write their own names and sometimes the names of important friends and family members.

Shows interest in developing large muscles

Four-year-olds use their large muscles to throw, climb, skip, hop, jump, catch, turn somersaults, and bounce. While they still are not as accurate as five-year-olds, they are much more skilled than three-year-olds. They tend to fall and trip but usually get up and try again throughout this year.

Social and Emotional Development

Is becoming more responsible

Older preschoolers start to follow simple classroom rules, such as cleanup, turn taking, and sharing. While they aren't always successful, they show more responsibility than three-year-olds.

Engages primarily in associative play

Four-year-olds are very social and interested in making friends instead of playing alone. They play alongside and with each other without clearly defined rules or roles.

Has an increasing attention span

Four-year-olds show a growing ability to follow directions and complete tasks, but they still may become sidetracked. They can pay attention for ten or more minutes while listening to stories, singing, playing group games, and cleaning up.

Is developing patience

Four-year-olds develop more patience and can wait for short periods of time to take turns, snack, go outside, and await story time or other planned activities.

Understands "boyness" and "girlness"

At this stage of development, preschoolers develop an awareness of their gender and the gender of those around them. Preschoolers often ask questions about gender issues.

Is developing friendships

Four-year-olds use language more than ever, and their endless chatter needs a target—someone with whom they can connect. Their social nature dictates that they build relationships with friends, however briefly.

Is becoming a perspective taker

Four-year-olds develop their awareness of the feelings of others. They can read emotions in peers and adults and make statements about others' feelings, such as "He is sad because he wants to see his mommy."

Engages in turn taking and in waiting

Once four-year-olds can read the feelings of their friends, they can wait their turn more easily. They can wait patiently while Jenni finishes a matching game, for example. Because rational thought is emerging, they can reason that Jenni will be finished soon and their turn will be next.

Engages in group play

Four-year-olds gravitate to peers in group play. They place greater importance on being in the same area of the classroom or playground with those they feel connected to.

Role-plays

Older preschoolers have active imaginations and like to make up stories and characters they can easily role-play. There are no definite rules except that all children keep their characters in play. They often reenact familiar experiences with important adults or those of TV characters.

Uses words to solve problems

Four-year-olds use words more often than physical aggression to express their anger or to sort out differences.

Shows fear

Four-year-olds begin to show fear of things like curtains moving in the dark, shadows on the wall, or unknown noises. They start to separate the real from the unreal and to learn about danger.

May use kiddie profanity

Phrases such as *poo-poo head* can be heard from preschoolers fascinated with language and experimenting with the effects that some words can have on adults and peers. Four-year-olds use words like *poopy* (which can be heard in just about any combination) to seek attention and test limits.

Communication and Language Development

Speaks in six- to ten-word sentences

Four-year-olds' sentence structures are much more developed than they were a year ago. Their ability to express more complex thoughts, such as "Can we go to the playground with my new ball today?" emerges.

Sings more complicated songs; enjoys fingerplays and rhymes

Four-year-olds can memorize words to familiar songs with lyrics that are repetitious.

Tells simple stories in sequence

Older preschoolers can now tell stories with beginnings, middles, and ends. They can narrow story events to logical sequences, such as "They went to the store and then went to the zoo and then went back home." They also use vocal expression and lots of gestures to provide clues about the world as they see it.

Spells name

At four, most children can spell their names, with an occasional reversal of letters. They quickly learn the letters in their names if they often have been exposed to their names in print.

Uses appropriate speech

Although four-year-olds use baby talk occasionally, their speech is very developed and understandable. They continue to make grammatical errors, but when adults model appropriate speech, they correct most of the errors by the end of the fifth year.

Follows three-step directions

Many four-year-olds can follow three-step directions, such as "Close the book and put it on the shelf and then bring your trucks over here to play." Their level of interest in the directions may affect their listening ability or their willingness to carry out the command.

Refers to *yesterday* and *tomorrow* correctly

Four-year-olds correctly use words for concepts of time, such as *yesterday* and *tomorrow*, when they learn to use language for thinking and communicating.

Knows first and last name

Older preschoolers have expanded their knowledge of names to include their last names. Many can tell you their middle names.

Pronounces words and sounds correctly

For the most part, four-year-olds can say or repeat the majority of the words they have heard. They may continue to have trouble with sounds such as "r," "th," "f," and "v," but each child is different and may take a little longer to perfect language sounds.

Uses pronouns in sentences

It is common for four-year-olds to use and overuse pronouns—*he/she*, *I/me*, *we/they*, and *you*—when they excitedly tell stories. Instead of saying, "The girl went to the store and got ice cream for her brother," they may say, "She went to the store and she got some ice cream for him." Four-year-olds often leave out necessary nouns (such as *girl* and *brother* in the example) or the names of story characters, replacing them with pronouns.

Cognitive Development

Begins to reason

Four-year-olds start to reason when they make decisions, understand, explain, predict, and even try to manipulate others to meet their own needs. Reasoning often occurs through play, because this is when preschoolers practice problem solving. "How many boys and girls can fit inside that box?" "What happens when you hit a friend?" "How much food does it take to feed all the ducks in the pond?" are questions four-year-olds ask as they try to reason.

Engages in more developed play themes

Four-year-olds start to extend their play themes based on their curiosity and backgrounds. Beginning with traditional themes like housekeeping or home play, four-year-olds move on to themes such as pets, birthdays, the beach, the post office, the zoo, and the farm, enriching their vocabularies and emerging literacy skills.

Understands simple concepts

Preschoolers understand simple concepts like age, number, size, weight, color, shape, texture, and distance:

Age: "I'm four, but my baby sister is one."

Number: "I have two turtles in my room."

Size: "I'm bigger than my dog."

Weight: "This is too heavy!"

Color: "You get all the brown ones, and I'll get all the red ones."

Shape: "Look at that big circle."

Texture: "I don't want to wear it 'cause it's too scratchy."

Distance: "My gramma lives a long way from here."

Sorts or categorizes items

Four-year-olds sort or categorize by attributes, such as size (big, medium, little), color, and shape (triangle, circle, square, rectangle). They can sort a variety of objects, noticing like-nesses and differences, a skill needed for prereading and premath.

Puts things in order or sequence

Four-year-olds can order objects from smallest to largest or largest to smallest. They can also understand the sequence of daily routines; for example, they expect adults to keep rest time after lunch and outside time after rest time.

Notices patterns

Older preschoolers start to notice and identify patterns in their environment. *ABABAB* and *red, blue, red, blue, red, blue* are the simplest pattern for four-year-olds and can be readily extended to *ABCABCABC* or *triangle, circle, square, triangle, circle, square, triangle, circle, square*. To make new patterns or to extend existing ones, four-year-olds must know how to compare as well as to order.

Counts objects out loud

During their fourth year, preschoolers can count between five and fifteen objects with few errors. As their sequencing skills develop, their numeracy skills increase too. They become more logical, knowing that the last number in an additive sequence is the greatest one.

Is interested in the alphabet

Four-year-olds know about half of the letters of the alphabet (upper and lower case), especially those used in writing their own names and the names of important others. They learn that letters represent written speech and that words can go together. They learn environmental print—that is, print that is everywhere around them—signs, books, and packaging, for example. When they go to the grocery store, signs such as "Apples $1.29 lb" may reinforce the lesson that knowing letters is necessary.

Is developing early literacy

Four-year-olds enjoy looking at and listening to books, scribbling and drawing on just about anything, telling stories to anyone who will listen, and recognizing a few words in print. Reading and writing can come later, but right now, caregivers' focus should be on providing a literacy- and language-rich environment so developing readers and writers can safely explore through rhythm, rhyme, song, and text. Reading, singing, telling stories, and writing with preschoolers instills a love for literacy.

Identifies colors

Four-year-olds have increased their color vocabulary/knowledge; they can identify more colors than they could a year ago. They are interested in color names like *fuchsia, watermelon, sky blue,* and *vermilion.* Their love of color and wordplay keep them interested in the whole box of sixty-four crayons.

Approaches to Learning

Works at tasks despite distractions and interruptions

By the age of four, children's attention spans have increased dramatically. Preschoolers can often work on the task at hand for a longer period of time without being distracted by every interruption.

Seeks and accepts help and information

At four, most children ask questions when they want help or information from trusted adults. They may ask such questions as "Can you tie my shoe?" and "Why do we have to clean up now?"

Offers ideas and suggestions

Preschoolers are problem solvers by nature. Adults can nurture this trait by engaging four-year-olds in conversation and asking them open-ended questions, such as "How can we . . .?" and "What do you think about . . .?"

Reflects on past experiences and applies information to new situations

When solving problems, four-year-olds say, "Last time, we took turns using the blue marker."

CHAPTER 9: FIVE-YEAR-OLDS

Often called *kindergartners,* five-year-olds develop in predictable patterns, at their own rates and in their own time. Their developmental milestones are usually met during windows or spurts of development. Cognitively, they are incredible thinkers and doers when their brains are stimulated by enriched environments and lots of concrete activities. They are much more self-sufficient and independent than four-year-olds and can make plans as well as carry them out. They make friends easily and enjoy playing simple group games that require rules. Their self-esteem develops when they enjoy success in the activities planned for them. Physically, they experience a lot of growth in their large and small muscles, which improves the gross- and fine-motor skills they use to play beginning sports and learn to write. With ever-increasing receptive and expressive vocabularies, five-year-olds increase their language skills rapidly.

One of the most important milestones for five-year-olds is developing the ability to think about what others think and feel. This ability is known as *perspective taking.* Perspective taking is a cognitive process. It is different from empathy, which is an emotional process. Five-year-olds are delightful to have in your care—they have high energy and are often funny, full of silly stories, and filled with creative expression. While the following developmental milestones are common by the end of age five, remember that all children develop at different rates.

Physical and Motor Development

Throws a ball to a target overhand and underhand
Throwing at a target encourages five-year-olds to develop their physical and motor skills. Many five-year-olds begin organized sports in which throwing is necessary, and they develop their large muscles when they pitch balls overhand and underhand.

Catches a ball when thrown or bounced
Five-year-olds increase their activity levels by playing with balls. Catching a soft, safe ball when it's thrown or bouncing a ball by themselves helps kindergartners improve their hand-eye coordination.

Balances well
Five-year-olds can walk on low balance beams, lines on the floor or the ground, play structures, and low ledges—anywhere they can practice balancing. Children of this age find pleasure in balancing; it is a forerunner to walking, running backward, and riding a bike.

Uses left or right hand with dominance

By this stage of development, children show a definite hand dominance or preference. Although hand preference is mostly genetic, once five-year-olds start using a particular hand to hold a fork, throw a ball, or paint a picture, adults should allow them to use their preferred hand.

Jumps over objects eight to ten inches high without falling

Jumping over cones or small barriers in an obstacle course, playing hopscotch, and jumping rope are fun activities to help children master balancing.

Uses large muscles to run, skip, tumble, kick a ball, and hop

Five-year-olds develop their large muscles through daily physical activities. Chores or class jobs can also help children develop their large muscles and may include sweeping, gardening, cleaning up the block center, and putting away the trikes.

Is learning to jump rope

Most five-year-olds can jump rope independently when they can control the speed of the rope. Jumping when others hold the rope comes later.

Is learning to tie shoes

Five-year-olds start tying their shoes.

Rides two-wheeler

By the end of kindergarten, most five-year-olds can ride two-wheeled bikes without training wheels.

Uses a tripod (three-finger) grasp

Five-year-olds can easily hold writing and painting utensils using a tripod grasp.

Social and Emotional Development

Takes turns and shares more easily

Five-year-olds are more skillful at taking turns than four-year-olds. Their impulse control has improved because they understand time concepts better. For example, they understand that *after* happens later than *now* and that they will get their turn after someone else has finished.

Plays simple games with rules

At this stage, children naturally think up games with rules during play. Such games can satisfy their need to connect while they move from independent play toward group play. As they learn more about themselves, their peers, and their environment, they can communicate more effectively with others.

Follows and makes simple rules

Five-year-olds are better at following rules about familiar things than four-year-olds. They sometimes participate in rule making, saying, "No hitting allowed—it hurts our friends" or "Use our inside voices when inside."

Often plays with peers

Five-year-olds are interested in having best friends and often exclude others ("You're not my friend, so I don't want you to play"). Although they sometimes sound cruel, they are learning to discriminate between their likes and dislikes in objects, experiences, and people.

Continues to play alone

Although most five-year-olds prefer to play with friends, they may also spend time playing alone, so caregivers should provide comfortable places, such as large cardboard boxes, soft cushions in out-of-the-way spots, or "by myself" tables or areas, for solitary play.

Shows strong emotions

Anger, excitement, and anxiety are common in kindergartners. They begin to learn how to deal with these strong feelings from adults who talk with them or model ways of coping.

Tries new things without much reservation

Five-year-olds are more daring and self-confident than four-year-olds and willingly try new experiences. Games that allow five-year-olds to be successful and that are not too competitive are ideal.

Responds to appropriate praise

When praise is used sparingly and tied directly to actions, five-year-olds respond positively. "You stacked those blocks on the shelf so they would not fall" is more appropriate than "You did a good job stacking those blocks."

Is self-directed

Five-year-olds commonly say, "I can do it myself." Respect their need to be self-directed and to engage in challenging activities that can be mastered with persistence.

Is sensitive to the feelings of others

Kindergartners may say, "Are you okay?" or "Miss Maggie, Janie needs help!" Five-year-olds often take action when a peer is hurt. Although they attend to their own friends' needs more readily, they are often sympathetic to all peers.

Shows strong connection to family, especially siblings

Kindergartners may say, "Daddy is going on a trip to Arizona, but he's coming back in two days!" or "My baby brother is having a birthday party. Want to come?" Five-year-olds are quick to talk about family events and appreciate efforts to feel connected to family while in care.

Communication and Language Development

Answers questions about familiar stories

Five-year-olds understand that stories have a beginning, middle, and end, can remember ideas from a story, and can retell it.

Speaks clearly and fluently; constructs sentences that include detail

"We went to the museum to see the ankylosaurus" says a five-year-old who has been regularly exposed to elaborate and extensive speech. Cultural values and the kinds of speech five-year-olds have been exposed to must be considered when this benchmark is measured.

Argues, reasons, and uses *because*

Many five-year-olds start to use reasoning in their arguments to make things fair or to understand the rules.

Makes up stories

Many children at this age create their own stories during sociodramatic or pretend play, devising roles or identities for themselves that guarantee them places in the play. Children may say, "I'm the fireman, and your house is on fire. You want me to put it out with water in my hose?"

Converses easily with adults

Talking to adults can be a great way for children to expand their vocabularies and to have meaningful conversations. Five-year-olds can learn the back-and-forth nature of conversation when adults set aside time to talk with and listen to them.

Has an expanding vocabulary

The number of words in kindergartners' vocabulary increases, and they use bigger, more sophisticated words appropriately. They may also use kiddie profanity or swearwords they have heard.

Uses language to control

Five-year-olds often feel the need to control activities and peers. Sometimes their attempts to lead are mistaken for bossiness. Children who develop more complex play with rules often try to boss their peers around to achieve compliance or agreement. Controlling others with language is more common in girls and children who are cognitively advanced.

Asks lots of questions

Five-year-olds are curious and want to understand more about how things work, so their many questions are understandable. "Why do the clouds float by?" and "Where do babies come from?" are important questions to five-year-olds.

Cognitive Development

Counts twenty or more objects with accuracy

Having learned the number sequence 1 to 10 or more, five-year-olds can now count real objects. They must organize objects so they won't forget which ones already have been counted. This takes memory skills as well as counting skills to do successfully.

Uses measurement terms

Five-year-olds use measurement terms in sentences, such as "That bus is really long," "My bike is so heavy that I dropped it," or "We went to soccer practice at six o'clock and didn't get home until late."

Understands *whole* and *half* and uses them in sentences

Five-year-olds can now distinguish a whole pizza from a half pizza and can use terms such as *whole, half,* and *one-fourth* in conversations.

Matches objects with ease

Sorting and matching activities using real objects helps satisfy children's need to match things in their environment.

Knows some names of coins and bills (money)

Five-year-olds learn and use the names of coins and bills while they play games or pretend scenarios that involve money and when they use money in real-life situations.

Estimates numbers in a group

Kindergartners can estimate small quantities (five to twenty) of objects in jars, boxes, canisters, etc.

Draws basic shapes and more

Drawing may be the creative language young children use to describe and connect to their world. They tend to draw what they see (shapes, for example), but they also draw as expressions of their reality (pets, home, the sun, family members).

Sorts and organizes

Five-year-olds can easily sort concrete objects. They are adept at sorting pictures and reading simple graphs too.

Expresses interest in creative movement

Kindergartners move their bodies like washing machines or pogo sticks because they know how things move and how their bodies can mimic those movements. They also listen and create movements to music and create movements about their feelings.

Approaches to Learning

Demonstrates openness to new learning

Kindergartners are curious by nature and love to learn new things. They are excited about learning and ask questions when experiencing new situations and circumstances.

Engages in play activities to demonstrate learning

Five-year-olds learn best through play-based activities, which teach them about themselves, their environment, other people, and the world around them.

Shows an increased ability to differentiate between reality and fantasy

By age five, children learn how to differentiate between fantasy and reality. They may begin to understand that trains and animals don't really talk and that there are not monsters living under their beds.

Develops an interest in the community and outside world

Kindergartners are interested in new experiences, the outside world, and their surrounding community. They begin to realize that many things happen around them and learn through their interactions with peers and adults.

Begins to organize information for remembering

Five-year-olds start to develop the ability to sort and organize information. As their brains develop, they can recall stored information and remember specific events.

CHAPTER 10: SIX-YEAR-OLDS

Six-year-olds are *young schoolagers*. They have left behind their preschool and kindergarten years and are now beginning formal schooling, attending either conventional elementary schools or homeschools. In the United States, most six-year-olds enter first grade. They engage in increasingly complex thinking and are task oriented. Their attention spans increase, and they enjoy working on projects and activities that take longer and require more thinking, exploration, and research. Six-year-olds are rule oriented and begin to make up more elaborate rules for the games they play. Their physical growth has slowed, their fine- and gross-motor coordination have improved, and their muscle strength has increased.

Six-year-olds especially enjoy playing and working with friends. They are less dependent on adults now that they make new friends and acquaintances. Their moods can swing suddenly. Six-year-olds use language nonstop and can talk to adults easily, asking many questions. Cognitively, they enjoy sensory play that includes manipulating materials and objects. They are drawn to puzzles and model building and to research and explore ideas that interest them.

Six-year-olds are individuals, and they start to understand the needs of others. Their play experiences are plentiful, rich, and full of curiosity, and their need to make friends is evident. While the following developmental milestones are common by the end of age six, remember that children develop at different rates.

Physical and Motor Development

Engages in vigorous physical/motor activity
To typically developing six-year-olds, running, jumping, somersaulting, throwing, kicking, climbing, hopping, and swinging are everyday events. As their balance and coordination improve, they can engage in more large-muscle activities.

Rides a bike without training wheels
Most six-year-olds have graduated from using training wheels on two-wheeled bikes. Their newfound steadiness gives them freedom and the ability to continue improving their coordination.

Ties shoelaces
In keeping with six-year-olds' ability to dress independently, they have mastered tying their shoes. This ability provides a new kind of autonomy.

Engages in fine-motor activity

Fine-motor activities, such as painting, cutting with scissors, modeling with clay, drawing, and woodworking, are important to six-year-olds. Developing their small muscles leads to new ways to express themselves through different media.

Writes numbers and letters with improving accuracy

Six-year-olds' improved fine-motor skills increase their ability to write. They also become more interested in printed words. Some numbers and letters are more difficult to write than others, and many six-year-olds practice diligently to perfect each one.

Prints name

Six-year-olds print their names with ease because they have left behind the scribbling stage of writing and are now proficient at forming letters to represent the names of important people and things. They understand the letters in their names better at this age than they did at age three or four, because now they know that letters are symbols for sounds.

Social and Emotional Development

Makes friends easily

Six-year-olds make and often break friendships. They learn important building blocks for socializing in adulthood when they practice being a friend, solving problems, and developing self-confidence.

Follows rules most of the time

Six-year-olds develop a sense of security when they have rules to follow. They invent rules where these are missing, and they remind peers about the rules to be followed.

Plays primarily with own gender

At age six, it is common for boys to play with boys and for girls to play with girls. Although this is not always the case, six-year-olds interact socially with peers of the same sex most of the time. This may be caused by young children's need for familiarity.

Develops perspective taking

Understanding the views (or perspectives) of others requires a lessening of six-year-olds' egocentric, or all-about-me feelings. When children are consumed by self-interest, they are unable to see beyond their own feelings. At age six, they start to take interest in others and to interact socially with them in positive ways. They practice the necessary perspective-taking skills they will need as adults.

Plays in groups

Group play helps young children learn to get along with others. It also teaches them about likenesses and differences in themselves and their peers. Six-year-olds naturally want to socialize, and play is a great arena for them to make the transition from associative play to more advanced, rule-based organized games and sports.

Displays many moods

Six-year-olds are often called moody because their feelings change frequently during play with peers when they try on many different roles. Usually their grumpiness lasts only a short while.

Completely dresses self

Six-year-olds can tie their shoes, brush their teeth, dress themselves, and zip up their coats. This newfound independence is exciting for them (and for adults as well).

Cares for belongings

At age six, children are much more capable of caring for their things. Once children can take responsibility for their possessions, there is much less stress for the caregiver and child. This is a major milestone for six-year-olds.

Communication and Language Development

Uses appropriate grammar

By this age, children have corrected many of their grammatical errors, such as "He goed to his grandma's house." Six-year-olds communicate with surprisingly perfect syntax (or sentence structure). When adults communicate with and read to children often, children's brains automatically interpret the rules of good sentence structure, and they begin to correct their own speech.

Asks a lot of questions

When six-year-olds come across something they do not know (called *a gap in knowledge*), they ask questions immediately, while they are most receptive to the answer. They do this from now throughout adulthood, increasing their cognitive development throughout life.

Tells stories (real and imagined)

Six-year-olds develop oral-language skills by listening to stories and then telling their own. Some of their stories are about real events, and some are made up. When telling stories, six-year-olds use a variety of voices, facial expressions, and gestures.

Engages in adult conversations

Six-year-olds enjoy conversations with adults because they can now use appropriate words and descriptions to hold the attention of adults.

Uses language to solve problems

As their vocabulary and reasoning skills increase, six-year-olds can solve problems with words instead of actions. Their language has become more sophisticated and their vocabularies have increased enormously.

Cognitive Development

Has an attention span of twenty to thirty minutes

Six-year-olds have longer attention spans and can sit for direct instruction in small doses.

Plays games with rules

Six-year-olds enjoy simple rules when they play board and card games with friends and adults. They are interested in fairness and are rule watchers much of the time.

Knows left from right

At age six, children know left from right but may occasionally make errors. Some children do not master this skill until age nine or ten.

Is aware of time

Although they may not tell time at age six, they are more time conscious and aware that some events start at certain times. They might say, "Is it eight o'clock, Mama? We have to get to school," or "Can I watch cartoons at five o'clock?" They may learn to tell time more easily with digital clocks, but an understanding of time sequence is not fully developed at this age.

Is aware of seasons

Six-year-olds know that winter may bring snow and certain holidays, that summer is often hot, and that fall can bring football games and trick-or-treating, but they are not ready for the abstract, scientific concepts about weather.

Counts past fifty

Many six-year-olds can count well past fifty, and some may count to 100 or more. They understand number sequencing and how numbers repeat in patterns.

Counts by twos, fives, and tens

Skip counting is common among six-year-olds. They learn to group numbers by twos, fives, tens, and more. One Hundred Days of School is a familiar first-grade activity teachers use to present the concept of 100. Six-year-olds bring collections of 100 items—such as buttons, marbles, small toys, or pennies—to school. They often skip count the items.

Decodes unknown words

Six-year-olds practice reading strategies when they figure out the meaning of unfamiliar words, using phonics and contextual clues, and put them together to read with understanding.

Sight reads

Six-year-olds become avid readers when they understand how print works and discover the value and enjoyment of reading. Their comprehension increases when they read stories and poems about topics that interest them.

Writes stories

As they learn the alphabet and spelling skills, six-year-olds begin to write stories that include things that are important to them, such as friends and family, family trips, and other events at home and at school. Invented or emergent spelling is common at this time and children write words with spellings that may not be standard. "I lik to pla bawl" is an example of invented spelling and does not interfere with the child's natural progress in learning to spell.

Identifies familiar money

Six-year-olds enjoy sorting familiar coins and paper money and using these to shop for well-earned rewards. Familiarity with coins—pennies, nickels, dimes, quarters, and dollars—comes from playing games, sorting, and exploring their properties as well as their value.

Knows simple fractions

Children as young as six are interested in taking things apart and putting them back together, becoming familiar with parts and wholes. Simple fractions, such as one-half and one-fourth, are easily mastered when children use real objects to discover the ways parts can make wholes. Many six-year-olds have already mastered halves and fourths and perhaps other fractions.

Understands simple addition and subtraction

Now that they know number concepts, or how many objects are grouped with each number, six-year-olds are ready to regroup numbers. Simple addition and subtraction problems with single digits are appropriate, and concrete objects are still important for introducing the concepts. "How many windows are in this room?" and "How many windows are on the door of this room?" are questions that can precede writing symbols for the number of windows: 5 windows + 1 window = 6 windows.

Creates and extends more complex patterns

Six-year-olds find complex patterns interesting. They can extend simple linear patterns, such as *ABABAB*, to *ABCDABCDABCD*, or even to *AABBCCAABBCC*. They can also recognize patterns in picture books, parking lots, and everyday routines, and on walls and buildings.

Identifies and draws simple two- and three-dimensional shapes

Although six-year-olds can already draw two-dimensional shapes, such as squares, triangles, circles, rectangles, and ovals, they can now identify and draw some three-dimensional shapes, such as cones, cubes, cylinders, and spheres.

Knows the days of the week

Six-year-olds have a beginning sense of order and can understand more complex patterning. These two concepts are important for understanding the days of the week and their recurrence. Younger children can name the days of the week in songs or by rote, but six-year-olds have gained an understanding of time and how weeks are structured around seven days.

Approaches to Learning

Seeks more information about topics or activities of interest

At age six, children have developed preferred interests and activities. As their sense of curiosity grows, six-year-olds actively seek out information from others about their preferred activities and interests.

Recognizes and seeks out new learning materials in the environment

When a learning environment contains new materials, six-year-olds notice. They enjoy new challenges and trying new things, so they recognize and seek out new learning materials.

Shows enthusiasm about trying new things: shows willingness to take risks in learning new skills

Six-year-olds show an increasing ability to take risks to learn new skills. By this age, they have experienced success in trying new things and are courageous when undertaking new tasks and adventures.

Demonstrates an ability to learn in structured and unstructured situations

By this age, children can learn in a variety of structures and unstructured situations. For example, they learn while attending school during the day and while playing outside with a sibling in the evening.

Understands the connection between behavior and consequences

Six-year-olds know that there are certain rules for every situation and that choosing to not follow those rules results in consequences.

CHAPTER 11: SEVEN-YEAR-OLDS

Seven-year-olds have become much more cooperative, sharing, and independent. Their individual traits start to shine, and the care and feelings they have for others become central to their being. Their need to follow rules began at age six, and this is even more important now, when they act more responsibly and take things more seriously. Seven-year-olds understand more about the world around them and about the concepts of life and death. Their fears often bring anxiety and feelings of dread, for example, about starting school, making friends, getting good grades, and losing people or pets they love.

The physical growth of seven-year-olds is slowing, with only small increases in weight and height. At this age, boys are usually taller than girls. Children are generally healthier at age seven than they were in their earlier years, but they still have minor illnesses, such as colds and fevers. Motor development continues to improve, and seven-year-olds often excel at playing sports or musical instruments. Their coordination improves, but their physical development lags behind their cognitive and social development.

Friends and family are important to seven-year-olds, who enjoy spending time with both. Their storytelling and story-writing abilities grow more sophisticated and include better-developed themes and plots. They continue to refine their language skills, enhancing their cognitive abilities and social interactions, and they begin to acquire play languages, such as pig Latin. Literacy takes the place of learning language structures: they become better writers and readers and learn new vocabulary.

Cognitively, seven-year-olds learn the concept of conservation (knowing that a quantity remains the same, even if its containers are different), an important milestone. They are still in Piaget's preoperational period of cognitive development and start to use symbols when they think about experiences outside of their current or past experience.

Seven-year-olds are funny, perplexing, tiring, sometimes demanding, enthusiastic, and fun. They need adults who are flexible and who understand their many moods and feelings, adults who will be there when they need assistance but who allow them to empower themselves. This is a year of cognitive and social and emotional growth. While the following developmental milestones are common by the end of age seven, remember that children develop at different rates.

Physical and Motor Development

Rides a bicycle with ease
Seven-year-olds have a keen sense of balance and can ride bikes without training wheels or assistance from adults. Bike riding without aids is an important milestone at this age.

Is involved in sports, dance, or other active play

Activities children choose can enhance their development, and children often choose activities in which they can excel. Physically, boys and girls have about the same strength, but choosing to play basketball or baseball or to take gymnastics, dance, or martial arts classes depends on their preferences and on the likelihood of their success. Body size, coordination, and energy level help seven-year-olds choose activities that are just right for them.

Runs up and down stairs with ease

Seven-year-olds tend to run up and down stairs, jumping over or skipping several stairs and landing with a thump at the bottom. Increased motor skills provide agility they have not had before.

Prints with ease

Fine-motor skills are required for printing and other school activities. Seven-year-olds frequently use their small muscles to cut with scissors, write stories, and draw and paint pictures.

Social and Emotional Development

Enjoys organized play or organized time with others

Gymnastics, baseball, swimming, jumping rope, and bike riding are a few of the outside group activities that seven-year-olds enjoy. Board and card games and projects that require teamwork help seven-year-olds develop social skills.

Enjoys solitary play or spending time alone

Seven-year-olds enjoy playing and working alone. Collecting things, such as trading cards, dolls, coins, action figures, rocks, and seashells, is a favorite pastime for children of this age.

Has frequent disagreements with peers

Seven-year-olds often have disagreements with peers, but their differences of opinion are typically not long lasting and require little intervention from adults or other peers. Seven-year-olds' emotions change quickly, and their need for friendships and to be liked helps children sort out their differences with peers. Seven-year-olds are impatient, often the cause of many arguments.

Can collaborate with peers

Once seven-year-olds begin to understand the actions of their playmates, they can collaborate and cooperate more.

Plays by the rules

At age seven, children want to be a part of a group and are willing to play by the rules in order to be accepted. As they begin to develop a moral sense, they start to look at issues in the world around them, such as hunger, homelessness, and war.

Communication and Language Development

Enjoys storytelling

Seven-year-olds have learned to think more logically and sequentially, and they can now tell stories with true beginnings, middles, and ends. Their stories include monsters, favorite animals, and life events. Telling stories stimulates creativity and imagination in young schoolagers and gives them a sense of pride and accomplishment when they can engage an audience.

Enjoys story writing

Seven-year-olds can now write stories that they make up, often with adult help. Story starters, such as word walls with scary words or keyword lists of important color and number words, often propel children to write stories on their own.

Is learning to spell words correctly

Though seven-year-olds once used pretend spelling to write their names and other words, they now understand that letters have sounds that go together to make meaning. They also know that a printed word is speech written down. After pretend spelling, they used invented spelling based on their understanding of letter-sound associations (*b* as in ball, for example), but it looked something like, "I luv mi dg." Now, at age seven, they are more fluent in spelling because they better understand phonemes (speech sounds).

Uses speech that is adultlike

Seven-year-olds use sentence structures and words that are understandable to adults. Often mimicking grown-ups, they use big words, such as *excellent* or *commotion*. Words like *family* and *birthday* are often called Tier 1 words (words that children naturally pick up as they develop and mature). Seven-year-olds also learn Tier 2 words, such as *temperature* and *coincidence,* when adults use them in context.

Cognitive Development

Reads with comprehension

Even though they are considered early readers, seven-year-olds now read for meaning. Children with highly developed vocabularies read and comprehend better. Children are more interested in reading when they are presented with books that are related to their own real-life, cultural experiences. Understanding printed words comes easiest for readers who can decode or sound out words and who can attach meaning to words while they are read.

Reads for pleasure

Seven-year-olds often read for enjoyment, besides reading for school assignments. Most of them have been exposed to adults who read for pleasure. Scary stories and chapter books about animals or overcoming obstacles are popular with them. Children who read for pleasure often go on to earn degrees and to communicate more effectively.

Tells jokes and riddles

Besides being just plain fun, telling jokes and answering riddles can also help children become better readers, ask questions, and use abstract thinking.

Shows interest in technology

Seven-year-olds show much skill using technology. While their screen time must be monitored, seven-year-olds can research topics and find information on subjects they are interested in online.

Shows interest in maps and globes

Seven-year-olds are interested in geography and use maps and globes to learn about people, places, climates, languages, and flags in their community and around the world. They also enjoy making maps because they now understand that maps' symbols stand for concrete objects.

Shows interest in simple graphs

Seven-year-olds can visualize information when they create graphs. Picture graphs and simple bar graphs are easy for seven-year-olds to construct and explain.

Knows months of the year

Seven-year-olds understand that the days of the week occur over and over again and transfer that knowledge to the months of the year.

Shows interest in current events

Seven-year-olds show a new interest in current events. These may be political or humane, such as presidential elections, world hunger, homelessness, and natural disasters.

Shows interest in history and prominent people

Seven-year-olds have a growing interest in social studies and the people who have shaped their country's government, such as U.S. presidents, governors, and significant events.

Measures objects

Once seven-year-olds master the concept of size, they are ready to take on more specific measurements. They can be introduced to inches and centimeters, and they enjoy using rulers and yardsticks to measure just about anything.

Is conscious of time

Seven-year-olds become aware of what time it is, can read digital clocks, and can report the time. They can also read analog clocks, telling time to the hour. Young schoolagers participate in more after-school activities and want to know when they will be picked up from their programs. They rely on clocks to keep themselves informed.

Approaches to Learning

Engages in play that is detailed and focused

Seven-year-olds often engage in dramatic play with elaborate plot lines, create art projects with multiple components, write made-up stories, and participate in other types of detailed and focused play.

Demonstrates learning through the construction of projects: creative development

At age seven, children have active imaginations and constantly use their creativity. They learn best by constructing projects, for example, putting together a Lego house with a friend or building a castle out of marshmallows.

Chooses, plans, researches, and expands on ideas

Once seven-year-olds develop more complex thinking, they can choose, plan, research, and expand on ideas, for example, creating a lemonade stand or hosting a dance party on the playground.

Uses language to clarify thinking and learning

Seven-year-olds have large vocabularies and the ability to think concretely. They can use language to clarify their thinking and learning, supported by conversations with peers and adults.

CHAPTER 12: EIGHT-YEAR-OLDS

Eight-year-olds are often referred to as *schoolagers* and can be the life of the party! Their outgoing personalities have blossomed, and they are clearly more interested in being with their peers than in being alone. Active eight-year-olds are constantly busy, hanging out with friends and trying new things. They are sensitive to criticism and respond to a firm yet democratic style of discipline. "If you clear the table, then you can watch TV" works better than "You can't watch TV unless you clear the table" or "Clear the table because that's what you're supposed to do."

Physically, eight-year-olds are full of energy and sometimes feel nothing is too hard for them. Their overall growth is slow but steady, and they look more mature and are generally healthier than they were at six or seven, contracting fewer childhood illnesses. Eight-year-olds expect more privileges, such as later bedtimes. Hormonal activity begins in boys and girls, and mood swings are common. Social competence in eight-year-olds is central to their need to make friends and to be friends. If they lack social skills, some children as young as eight may begin to bully and have difficulty getting along with others. This is a favorable age at which to teach children the etiquette skills they need to become sociable.

Eight-year-olds' language skills are well developed, and they can write and speak correctly. However, because children's cultures differ, their competence shouldn't be judged without considering the language they use and understand best. Cognitively, eight-year-olds can manage difficult situations with peers verbally.

During this year, children make progress in concrete operations, meaning that they can better think with symbols. They can see things from different perspectives. While the following developmental milestones are common by the end of age eight, remember that children develop at different rates.

Physical and Motor Development

Shows good body coordination
Eight-year-olds throw at targets with accuracy and are agile, steady, swift, and strong when playing sports, riding bikes, swimming, jumping rope, dancing, or participating in martial arts.

Has an expanded attention span
Eight-year-olds can sit for longer periods of time (about 30 minutes) but need to have a lot of hands-on, interactive experiences and a schedule that balances vigorous and quiet activities throughout the day.

Shows good hand-eye coordination

Eight-year-olds hold writing tools, such as pencils, with more precision and less tension. They can draw straight lines, write in cursive, sketch, draw, and paint because their fine-motor skills improve throughout this year.

Engages in high-energy activities

Soccer, baseball, basketball, tennis, swimming, gymnastics, and karate require a lot of strength. Eight-year-olds often choose these sports to burn off energy.

Builds and takes things apart

Concrete thinking allows eight-year-olds to think forward (to build things) and in reverse (to take things apart). Computers, radios, phones, video recorders—just about anything with parts—interest eight-year-olds.

Social and Emotional Development

Engages in group over solitary play

Group play that includes clubs and teams is important to eight-year-olds. They need to be part of a group much more than they need to be alone at this age. Clubs or teams for scouting, swimming, reading, tennis, board games, cooking, volunteering, music, art, and academics are popular among eight-year-olds.

Is influenced by peer pressure

Eight-year-olds use peer pressure to get others to conform or to come along with them. If they urge someone to join an after-school club that puts baskets of food together for homeless children, then they direct pressure toward a positive end. But if they put pressure on someone to try smoking, to visit inappropriate sites on the Internet, or to join a group that routinely breaks rules, the outcome can be very negative.

Works and plays without becoming overly upset by results

Eight-year-olds can manage their feelings when they do not succeed or win.

Shows independence and tries new things

Eight-year-olds are curious and try new things. When they strive for independence from adults, they sometimes make choices that are distressing.

Experiences anxiety or fear

Eight-year-olds may worry about things to come and show frustration or symptoms of stress but refrain from discussing their fears with adults.

Plays solitary games

Solitaire, sudoku, puzzles, computer games, and handheld video games are some of the solitary favorites of eight-year-olds. Screen time should be monitored, and card games and puzzles encouraged. Because occasional solitary play is to be expected from eight-year-olds, children who engage in solitary games from time to time should not be confused with children who withdraw from group play or who do not have the social skills necessary to join groups.

Seeks love and compassion from others

Eight-year-olds need a lot of love and kindness from adults and peers. Typically developing eight-year-olds give affection and want it in return. They need to trust the adults who care for them and to feel they can take risks without losing the bonds they have with others.

Seeks adult approval

While seeking their own independence, eight-year-olds also seek adult support and approval. They need rules and boundaries and expect adults to set them. They also need praise, but only when it is performance based.

Communication and Language Development

Converses on an adult level

During this year, children sharpen their use of spoken language and can carry on conversations with most adults. Sentence structure has improved, and an increased expressive vocabulary enables most eight-year-old children to use culturally and grammatically correct speech.

Adjusts language to match audience

To meet their needs, eight-year-olds commonly use pragmatics or persuasive language with inflection and gestures when talking. They use different speech when talking to peers than to adults. They also use different speech on different occasions. For example, they'll use more formal speech at a spelling match and less formal speech on the playground.

Uses descriptive language

Eight-year-olds use descriptive and figurative language when they make comparisons: "My dad is a rocket on the basketball courts." They also use similes in sentences: "She swims like a fish." They use alliteration when they repeat initial consonant sounds: "He is as cool as a cucumber." Although they may not understand these terms, they fill their conversations with colorful and imaginative language.

Plays jokes on others and loves humor

Eight-year-olds use every opportunity to connect with peers and adults through humor. They play jokes often and use this harmless way of socializing to increase communication and be creative.

Uses language to express feelings and emotions

Expressing feelings verbally is a developing trait in school-age children. Eight-year-olds are sometimes brutally honest when they need to let others know how they feel. Children who are more verbal and those with larger vocabularies have the easiest time expressing feelings. They may say things like "I don't like it when you call me names" or "I'm really mad at you for cutting in line."

Uses slang

Dude, whoa, get out of here, awesome, and *peace out* are slang terms eight-year-olds use to express themselves to friends and peers. Sounding cool is important to eight-year-olds, who often mimic their older siblings and TV celebrities.

Uses abbreviated language in writing, such as TTYL (talk to you later) and LOL (laughing out loud)

Many eight-year-olds are accomplished instant messengers and e-mail users and use abbreviations such as *RUOK* for *Are you okay?*, *BTW* for *by the way,* and *BFF* for *best friend forever.*

Cognitive Development

Engages in projects

Eight-year-olds like to explore real-world events and topics in books, on field trips, and online. They learn best through hands-on activities and like to build models or conduct experiments rather than listen to someone talk.

Uses the calendar

Schoolagers are able to sequence numbers to 1,000 and beyond. Making and reading calendars is easy at this age. Many eight-year-olds are involved in after-school activities and sports and use calendars to mark weekly and monthly events to keep their parents apprised.

Engages in basic research

Observing, exploring, asking questions, and recording information are common to eight-year-olds. They become interested in particular topics and need to know more. Process is more important than product to many eight-year-olds.

Uses reasoning

Eight-year-olds' thinking becomes more logical and organized, and they need to know why things happen. They often ask questions to understand adult decisions or why things happen. Complex topics such as war or poverty are difficult for them to understand.

Shows interest in places and other cultures

Eight-year-olds are now aware that the world is filled with children like them in many ways but who are also different. Connecting with pen pals, visiting Internet sites with global perspectives, and learning about customs and habits of people in other lands are activities that interest eight-year-olds.

Shows interest in technology

A heightened interest in technological devices is very common among eight-year-olds. Their knowledge of technology and how it works astonishes many adults. They navigate the Web with ease. Working with technology in pairs, children learn valuable lessons in team-work and shared responsibility.

Approaches to Learning

Shows curiosity about nature, people, customs, and other countries

Eight-year-olds are increasingly curious about the world around them. As they continue to define their sense of self, they notice those around them and become curious about their differences.

Shows interest and curiosity in art, words, and actions

During this year, children develop increased interest in art, words, and actions, including the creation of art, books, and writing, as well as social interactions with peers.

Considers the perspectives of others; includes culture, race, ethnicity, and abilities when making group or individual decisions

Eight-year-olds are less egocentric than some of their younger peers. They can extend their thinking and use empathy, considering the perspective of others, when making decisions.

Shows persistence with minimal adult encouragement

By age eight, children have developed persistence when it comes to activities. Unlike younger children, eight-year-olds need little adult encouragement and can persist on their own.

Begins to reflect on learning and evaluates own learning

Eight-year-olds can begin to reflect on their own thinking and learning. Their knowledge base continues to expand because they can build upon their previous ideas and thoughts.

RESOURCES

Charts of Developmental Milestones

Charts of developmental milestones are plentiful online. Here is a compilation of useful ones.

Birth to 24 months

PBS Parents. 2015. "Baby & Toddler Milestones." Public Broadcasting Service (PBS). Accessed September 15, 2015. www.pbs.org/parents/child-development/baby-and-toddler/baby-toddler-milestones/

Birth to four years old

Department of Health, Government of South Australia. 2013. "Milestones: Children 0–4 Years." Women's and Children's Health Network. Accessed September 15, 2015. http://cyh.com/HealthTopics/HealthTopicDetails.aspx?p=114&np=122&id=1906

Georgia Department of Early Care and Learning. 2015. "Developmental Milestones." Bright from the Start. Accessed September 15, 2015. (Each milestone type connects to a different link): http://decal.ga.gov/ChildCareServices/ParentChildDevelopment.aspx

Birth to six years old

University of Washington Leadership Education in Neurodevelopmental and Related Disabilities. "Developmental Milestone Chart." University of Washington. Accessed September 15, 2015. http://depts.washington.edu/lend/pdfs/Developmental_Milestone_Chart_BEDavis.pdf

Birth to eight years old (includes suggestions for encouraging achievement of these milestones)

Beyond the Journal. 2004. "Children's Developmental Benchmarks and Stages: A Summary Guide to Appropriate Arts Activities." NAEYC (National Association for the Education of Young Children). Accessed September 15, 2015. http://journal.naeyc.org/btj/200407/ArtsEducationPartnership.pdf

Birth to 13+ years old

NSW Department of Community Services. 2008. "Developmental Checklist for Parents." New South Wales Government. Accessed September 15, 2015. www.community.nsw.gov.au/docswr/_assets/main/documents/par_development.pdf

Birth to 16 years old

Metropolitan Community College–Omaha. "Developmental Milestones for Children."
Accessed September 15, 2015. http://faculty.mccneb.edu/JFAUCHIER/psy121jf/Projects_
SS04/Jenni%20Powers/PSY121jf/milestones.html

Infant to six years old

Department of Education and Early Childhood Education, Victoria. 2007. "Your Child's Health
and Development: Birth to 6 Years." State Government of Victoria: Department of Education
& Training. Accessed September 15, 2015. www.education.vic.gov.au/Documents/childhood/
parents/health/chlchart6years.pdf

Infant through eight years old

Child Developmental Institute. 2015. "Language Development in Children." Accessed
September 15, 2015. http://childdevelopmentinfo.com/child-development/
language_development/

Two months to five years old (available in Spanish and English)

Centers for Disease Control and Prevention. 2015. "Developmental Milestones."
Accessed September 15, 2015. www.cdc.gov/ncbddd/actearly/milestones/

It's Been 20 Years

Fergus

(and you're still spooking at that thing?)

Jean Abernethy

Foreword by Dr. Robert M. Miller

TRAFALGAR SQUARE
North Pomfret, Vermont

First published in 2020 by
Trafalgar Square Books
North Pomfret, Vermont 05053

Disclaimer of Liability

The author and publisher shall have neither liability nor responsibility to any person or entity with respect to any loss or damage caused or alleged to be caused directly or indirectly by the information contained in this book. While the book is as accurate as the author can make it, there may be errors, omissions, and inaccuracies.

Trafalgar Square Books encourages the use of approved safety helmets in all equestrian sports and activities.

Library of Congress Cataloging-in-Publication Data

Names: Abernethy, Jean, author, illustrator.

Title: It's been 20 years Fergus : (and you're still spooking at that
    thing?) / Jean Abernethy ; foreword by Dr. Robert M. Miller.

Other titles: Fergus. Selections

Description: North Pomfret, Vermont : Trafalgar Square Books, 2020. |
    Summary: "Author and illustrator Jean Abernethy created Fergus, the
    world's most famous cartoon horse, 20 years ago. In this collection of
    comics, Fergus fans, young and old, get a glimpse of how his horsey
    humor has evolved since the publication of the last book of Fergus
    comics: The Essential Fergus the Horse"-- Provided by publisher.

Identifiers: LCCN 2020030493 | ISBN 9781570769580 (paperback)

Subjects: LCSH: Horses--Comic books, strips, etc. | American wit and humor,
    Pictorial.

Classification: LCC PN6728.F444 A35 2020 | DDC 741.5/973--dc23

LC record available at https://lccn.loc.gov/2020030493

Book and cover design by RM Didier
Typefaces: Source Serif Pro and Tally Text

Printed in China

10 9 8 7 6 5 4 3 2 1